P·38
LIGHTNING

Jesse Alexander

Motorbooks International
Publishers & Wholesalers ®

To
Duke Vincent

First published in 1990 by Motorbooks International
Publishers & Wholesalers, P O Box 2, 729 Prospect Avenue,
Osceola, WI 54020 USA

Motorbooks International books are also available at
discounts in bulk quantity for industrial or sales-promotional
use. For details write to Special Sales Manager at the
Publisher's address

Library of Congress Cataloging-in-Publication Data
Alexander, Jesse.
    P-38 Lightning : the restoration of a classic American warbird /
Jesse Alexander.
        p.   cm.
    ISBN 0-87938-441-7
    1. Lightning (Fighter planes)—Conservation and restoration.
I. Title.
UG1242.F5A364 1990
358.4'3—dc20   90-5957
                                         CIP

On the front cover: Fully restored and freshly painted, *Joltin'
Josie* takes wing. *Michael O'Leary*

On the back cover: In the crowded yard at Fighter Rebuilders,
a fork lift positions the P-38's port wing prior to installation.

Printed and bound in the United States of America

On the frontispiece: Joltin' Josie *is a P-38J-20-LO,
serial number 44-23314, Lockheed number 4318,
delivered to the Army Air Force in mid 1944. After the war,
it was purchased by a flight school and then sold to a
collector. John Maloney bought the P-38 from the collector for less than $2,000 and put it on static display at
his Planes of Fame Museum. After more than twenty years
on display, it was pushed into the hangar at Fighter
Rebuilders for a complete restoration. Restoration complete, the P-38 flew again, for the first time in over 25
years, on July 22, 1988.*

On the title page: *Tony LeVier took a P-38 to the 1946
Thompson Trophy Race. It's said that he put scotch tape
over the cracks in the airplane in an effort to clean up its
aerodynamics.* Bowers via Roger Huntington

Contents

Acknowledgments 6

Foreword 7

Introduction 11

1 **Chino and Fighter Rebuilders** 13

2 **Lockheed and Its Lightning** 28

3 **The Lightning Goes to War** 39

4 **The Restoration of *Joltin' Josie*** 56

5 **First Flights** 127

6 **On to Oshkosh** 150

Acknowledgments

I wish to thank a number of people without whose help this book would not have been possible.

First on the list is Steve Hinton and his crew at Fighter Rebuilders who welcomed me day in and day out. Thank you, guys.

I also would like to thank Tom Huston, who joined me on my frequent trips to Chino, California, and who never failed to find a new angle or vantage point from which to shoot a picture of the P–38.

Thanks to Duke Vincent, who alerted me to the project, and to H. N. "Pete" Madison of the 475th Fighter Group who helped tremendously with historical material.

Special thanks to John Kagihara and Rich Palmer, P–38 rebuilders whose explanations of the complex technical details associated with the rebuild were invaluable when it came time to produce captions and text.

Thanks to Col. Charles H. MacDonald, who welcomed me to his home in Florida and spent time talking with me about his experiences in the cockpit of *Putt Putt Maru*. Thank you, Mac.

Thanks to Tony LeVier, "Nick" Nicholson, Erik Miller and Eric Schulzinger, all from Lockheed, who gave generously of their time.

Fighter Rebuilders crew on the Lockheed P–38:
Bill Barclay
Jim "JP" Dale
Kevin Eldridge
Mark Foster
John Hinton
Steve Hinton
John "JK" Kagihara
John Maloney
Mike "Maj" McDougall
Mike "Lefty" McGuckian
Matt Nightingale
Rich Palmer
Alan Wojciak
Dennis Collins

Fighter Rebuilders wishes to thank the following for their help with the rebuild of the Planes of Fame P–38:
A.G. Lagne
Adel Company
Aero Trader
Air Museum Advisory Board
Airtreads
John Benjamin
Bowman Plating
Consolidated Aeronautics
Sam Davis
Dzus Fasteners Company
Excello Plating Company, Inc.
Tom Garagliano
Garrett Airesearch
Stephen Grey
Honeywell Corporation
Dave Horn
JRS Enterprises
Ed Kaletta
Korry Electronics
Lewis Engineering
Lord Manufacturing Company
John MacGuire
Dick Martin
Menasco Overhaul
Mikron Products
Bob Nightingale
Don Pennington
Bob and Jo Pond
R.B. Sales
Sanders Aircraft
Cherry Fasteners (Townsend Division of Textron)
Tearo, Inc.
Texas Instruments
Tube Sales, Inc.

Special thanks to Rex Barber, John Mitchell, I. Newton Perry, Ed Maloney of Planes of Fame and Jonathan Thompson.

I would like to thank Stan Stokes for supplying photographs of the P–38's flight to Oshkosh, Wisconsin, and to Jeff Brouws who made the black and white prints for the book.

Thanks to Joe Haley who gave me my first warbird ride, and to Nancy Alexander for her part in making the text readable.

I would like to offer my special thanks to Greg Field, aviation editor at Motorbooks, for his patience and his editorial skills which have made a significant contribution to this book.

Jesse Alexander
Carpinteria, California 1990

Foreword

Fifty years ago two memorable events took place, marking both the good and the bad of man's quest for achievement.

In America, a relatively small but famous aircraft company called Lockheed designed and built a revolutionary new kind of fighter-interceptor that would set the pace for all future military aircraft designs. It first flew on Jan. 27, 1939; the twin engine aircraft was to be the P–38 Lightning.

In Europe, in September 1939, Hitler started World War II by invading Poland, a country ill-prepared to defend itself against the onslaught of the Nazi blitzkrieg.

At the time, I was a 26 year old pilot at the Cleveland National Air Races. I was flying the world's fastest racer powered by a 550-cubic-inch engine; it was capable of speeds in excess of 350 miles an hour.

The news of the outbreak of World War II galvanized every one of us at those national air races. Most of the pilots offered their skills to the aircraft industry. I first went to Douglas Aircraft Company in Santa Monica, California, with hopes for a job as a test pilot. The test pilot job did not materialize fast enough for me, so I became co-pilot with Mid-Continent Airlines out of Kansas City, Missouri. With war clouds hanging over the entire European continent, Charles F. "Boss" Kettering of the General Motors Research Laboratory hired me to test his new secret engine to power a "buzz-bomb," a device he conceived during the First World War, then called the "doodle-bug."

It was here in the great GM Laboratories Division that I came in contact with the formidable new Allison V–12 aircraft engine that had powered the new Lockheed super fighter designed by C. L. "Kelly" Johnson in Burbank, California.

Allison, a division of GM, was fraught with all sorts of problems, most of which concerned the design of the engine's crankshaft and connecting rod. It was here that I witnessed tests being conducted to fix the fault. The crankshaft torsional vibration could destroy or break a crankshaft in a matter of minutes if the design were faulty; the same for the connecting rods being stretched in a massive machine.

Fate guided me to join the Lockheed Corporation as a test pilot on April 29, 1941. It was here I came in contact with the P–38 Lightning fighter being developed for the U.S. Army Air Corps. I had read about the P–38 and its incredible performance of climb and speed, but you had to fly it to believe it.

Late in the day on Feb. 5, 1942, several pilots were languishing about Lockheed flight operations, hoping to be released to go home or to the local bar for the usual daily libations to steady the nerves. Suddenly a P–38 was signed off for a test flight. No one wanted the flight. John Myers, one of Lockheed's senior test pilots, elected that they should check out Tony LeVier. This was a surprise to me, and with little or no knowledge of how to operate the P–38, I was not inclined to accept this new experience—but I didn't have the guts to admit it. I was hustled off to the flight line and promptly plunked into the P–38's seat and given a quick and dirty check-out.

The flight went off with no problems, but I was not comfortable because of lack of knowledge of the plane's systems and operating procedures. This bothered me to the extent that I took the P–38 pilot's operating manual home that night and read it from cover to cover. The next morning I was first to arrive at Lockheed flight operations and with my name on the top of the list, I was assigned to test fly the first P–38 signed off for flight that morning. As the saying goes, "It was love at first flight." In my case, it was on the second flight. I was lucky; a second P–38 was again signed off in late afternoon, and I got it.

The P–38 in 1942 was an outstanding fighter in every respect, but at the same time it was plagued with numerous problems that had no immediate answer. The worst of the problems was the "compressibility effect," which would cause the P–38 to nose over into a dive at high altitude, from which recovery would be extremely difficult, and, in some cases, impossible. Other problems included the Allison engine and its propensity to explode. This was caused by detonation, a violent explosion within the combustion chamber.

In early 1942, Kelly Johnson, Lockheed's aeronautical aircraft designer and creator of the P–38, was beset with demands to hire a test pilot with top credentials from outside Lockheed. The Air Corps

Tony LeVier, retired Lockheed test pilot, in his office at Burbank, California. He has flown virtually all of Lockheed's production aircraft, including the F-104 and the

U-2. He is known as Mr. P-38 for the countless hours he spent during the war in the development of the Lightning.

and the industry thought Lockheed didn't know what was going on, when in actuality, Johnson was more aware of the problems than the so-called experts. After an ill-conceived order to hire an outside test pilot, who had no idea whatsoever how to solve the then existing compressibility problem, Kelly demanded that the "outsider" be fired, and at the same time pleaded with Lockheed president Robert Gross to let him pick the pilots of his choice to do his P-38 flight testing. It was then, in June 1942, that Kelly selected Milo Burcham, Joe Towle, Jim White and me for what was to become one of the most famous organizations in world aviation history, the "Lockheed Skunk-Works."

My introduction into the big time came with a flourish and a loud explosion. I was assigned to take a P-38 up to 10,000 feet and pull the maximum Gs possible. It was during the 300–mph test point at 6½ Gs that the canopy above my head broke loose and blew away. The wind and noise were fierce! The results of the test: design a new canopy that would stand the explosive loads.

With the baptism of that event, I was cast into the role of testing Allison engines. Every flight

always included climbing to high altitude, pulling the maximum power that was allowed. These tests resulted in numerous engine explosions and complete destruction. All told, I personally have had 14 Allison engines blow up and break—but never more than one at a time.

Gradually the Allison engine became more reliable, and by the end of the war it was considered one of the best aircraft powerplants in the world.

Having been the fastest and highest climbing fighter plane in the world at the outset of WWII, the P-38 might have been, in retrospect, to our disadvantage. A new term called Mach Number appeared. It would alter the aerodynamic sciences dealing with speed all through the war years and well into the jet age which was soon to follow.

Mach Number, the relation of the speed of the airplane to that of the speed of sound, would soon become the watch word to fighter pilots of WWII, especially to those flying high altitude missions. We at Lockheed, being first to encounter "Mach-tuck," the tendency for the plane to nose over into uncontrollable dives, were first to discover what was causing the problem; and with the help of Gen. Henry

Tony LeVier raced this P-38 in the 1946 and 1947 Thompson Trophy races. He finished second in 1946 and fifth in 1947. Bowers via Roger Huntington

"Hap" Arnold, commanding officer of the U.S. Army Air Corps, we were able to discover what was going on after putting a P-38 model in the NACA (National Advisory Committee for Aeronautics) high-speed wind tunnel. The solution was the invention of the first dive flaps on a fighter plane. Milo Burcham, my boss, and I conducted the first compressibility dives in aviation history, and I made the last and final dive on P-38s to prove the dive flaps' success.

At the same time, we had another vexing problem P-38 fighter pilots complained about: the very heavy aileron forces necessary to roll the plane. The roll was an important maneuver to a fighter pilot, and I'll always remember the times that I would be sent up to record the rate of roll—only to throw my shoulders out of joint. I finally complained to Kelly Johnson; "Kelly you're wrecking my shoulders with these tests." Kelly thought for a minute and exclaimed, "We'll do something about that and power-boost the ailerons." We did, and the P-38 became the first fighter in the world to have power-boosted controls (ailerons). We could now out-roll any fighter in the world. Along with two counter-rotating Allison engines, with concentrated 50-caliber machine guns and a 20 mm cannon, all centered out of the nose, the P-38 had the most devastating firepower of any fighter—in either the Allied or enemy air forces.

After WW II, thousands of war planes were put up for sale at prices of about one cent on the dollar value. I had always said, "When the war ends, I'm going to buy a P-38 and demonstrate it to America to show what a great plane it is; also to race it at the Cleveland National Air Races."

I became the first person to own a P-38 and my dream became a reality beyond belief. At the first post-WWII Cleveland National Air Races, I startled the aviation world with vertical dives with both engines feathered and doing a series of maneuvers to a dead engine landing. This was followed by winning second place in the Thompson Trophy Race against the world's best fighters.

Now, more than fifty years since the first P-38 took to flight, Jesse Alexander brings to aviation historians and buffs an account of the restoration of indomitable Lockheed P-38 Lightning fighter—the "Forked Tail Devil" the German Nazi pilots called it. It was the first WWII Allied fighter able to escort bombers to Berlin and return to Britain. It fought in every theater in WWII with devastating effect upon the enemy. It sank more Japanese shipping than all other fighters combined. It was an absolute terror in the skies of the Pacific war. America's leading ace was Maj. Richard Bong, with 40 victories, all with the P-38.

The P-38 Lightning lives on in this extraordinary and historical account of a great aircraft. It did its job with a combination of grace and fury. There was no other plane like it. I highly recommend Jesse Alexander's book *P-38 Lightning* for an exciting account of aviation history.

Tony LeVier

9

Returning from a test flight, this P-38 is photographed over Ventura, California. In the background are the Channel Islands. The Lockheed photographer often went along on test flights, whether it was a bomb run, a strafing run, a radio test session—whatever the PR director requested. Erik Miller

Introduction

Of all the fighter planes of World War II, the Lockheed P–38 Lightning was my particular favorite. The airplane's unique shape, with its twin-boom, twin-engine configuration and the pilot sitting amidships in his capsule, has always been an exciting visual experience. Just looking at the airplane is a turn-on. The two massive V–12 Allison engines mark it as a powerhouse, and the airplane is truly a landmark design by Lockheed's C. L. "Kelly" Johnson.

I saw my first P–38 Lightning at the age of twelve. World War II was well under way and I was visiting friends in Burbank, California, Lockheed's home. From the house where I was staying in the foothills of the San Fernando Valley, I had an excellent view of the factory. Production was in full swing not only for P–38s and Hudson bombers but also for Lockheed Vegas and B–17s. The noise of aircraft engines on the ground and in the air was constant. Below me, row after row of aircraft were parked and the sprawling factory dominated the landscape.

Smog was of no concern then, except for the occasional period in mid-winter when citrus growers turned on their smudge pots, and the Lockheed test pilots took advantage of the fine flying weather.

Erik Miller, who photographed for Lockheed during the war, told me that at one point there was a P–38 coming off the line every hour. Once the early bugs were ironed out the Lightning went on to spectacular successes, especially in the Pacific war against the Japanese. From a teen-ager's viewpoint it was fascinating and like everyone else of my generation, I expressed my love for those warbirds by drawing pictures of them, making models and collecting memorabilia, including posters, magazine clippings and Army Air Corps shoulder patches, all of which went into scrapbooks still on my shelves.

I had not seen a P–38 in many years, or even thought of one, until my son and I went to the annual Confederate Air Show at Harlingen, Texas. The highlight of the show was a flying demonstration by Lefty Gardner who flies a red, white and blue P–38 at air shows around the country. A few months later, a friend of mine, Duke Vincent, told me that a P–38 was being restored at the Planes of Fame Air Museum at Chino, California, by Steve Hinton's Fighter Rebuilders. Vincent had helped put together some of the funding for the plane's restoration, and he urged me to go out to Chino to have a look. I did just that and this book is the result.

The entrance to Chino Airport on Euclid Avenue in Chino, California, is marked by this sign which advertises the Planes of Fame Air Museum and restaurant, Flo's Cafe (famous for its biscuits and gravy).

Chapter 1

Chino and Fighter Rebuilders

Less than an hour's drive east of Los Angeles is Chino Airport, home of the Planes of Fame Air Museum and Fighter Rebuilders, a company founded in 1981 by Steve Hinton, Jim Maloney and a small group of their friends to restore World War II warplanes. Chino is "warbird country," with a number of other restoration shops at the airport. Warbirds of all shapes and sizes can be seen parked within the boundaries of the sprawling field that served as a training base during World War II.

B–17s, several B–25s, a Sea Fury, a Corsair or two, P–51s, even a covey of MiGs are mixed in amongst the general aviation scene. These are just a few examples of what you will see there on any given day. One memorable day as I was approaching the museum a beautifully restored Ford Trimotor trundled by so closely that the shadow of its wing passed over the top of my car. Chino is laid out like a jumbo-sized mini-storage complex with hundreds of privately owned hangars, many of which house interesting aircraft. A visit to Chino is never without a surprise because you never know what you are going to stumble across.

Fighter Rebuilders is located on the premises of the Chino air museum on the north side of the airport. The road to the airport passes a large number of dairy farms and in a way prepares you for the trip back into time; much of the architecture is left over from the 1930s and 1940s.

Pulling into the museum's parking lot, you cannot help but immediately notice two imposing relics of World War II: a dusty B–17 parked on the left, and on the right the tattered fuselage of a B–50. Music from the 1940s is played over a radio speaker as you enter the small gift shop at the main entrance. A video tape from a past Chino air show plays on a monitor nearby. Passing through the shop, you find yourself in a courtyard with a large hangar on one side and another building straight ahead. Aircraft are everywhere, both inside and out, all in various states, some in flying condition, some not.

Within a few minutes it is clear that this place contains an extraordinary collection of airplanes, all due to the foresight and dedication of one man, Edward T. Maloney, director of the air museum. He had the good sense to begin collecting World War II

airplanes immediately after the war. His life has been dedicated to not only acquiring the aircraft but seeing that whenever possible they are put back into flying condition.

To this end, Fighter Rebuilders was established in 1981 by Steve Hinton, the late Jim Maloney, Kevin Eldridge and several others. They all had been around planes ever since they could remember and had been involved in aircraft maintenance. They learned their craft by trial and error. Hinton characterizes himself as "a 'victim' of being in the right place at the right time. The only thing I had ever done," said Hinton, "was aircraft maintenance. Our first job was putting together a P–40 for Flying Tigers. They were attempting to restore this plane that they had acquired and had gotten in over their heads on the project, putting an immense amount of time and money into their airplane. They came to us to see if we could finish what they had started."

Hinton, a native of China Lake, California, grew up with planes, knowing early on that he wanted to be a pilot. He and Jim Maloney met in second grade, becoming friends because they both loved to draw airplanes. "Jim could draw planes better than I could," said Hinton. Maloney's father, Ed, owned the air museum which was then in Claremont, California, and it was a natural place for the two boys to share their common interest.

Planes of Fame moved to Chino Airport in 1973 and the collection has grown remarkably. Today there are more than seventy airplanes on display. One of the more valuable planes is the last remaining flyable Japanese Zero fighter. The plane is totally original and rumor has it that Ed Maloney has turned down a number of offers from interested Japanese collectors. Although not all of the warbirds at Planes of Fame are in flying condition, a few are and a visitor to the museum, particularly on a weekend, will undoubtedly be treated to the sight and sounds of these aircraft in action. Planes of Fame offer rides in a P–51 Mustang, and for a donation to the museum an experienced pilot will take you for an unforgettable ride.

Not only has the museum's collection grown, but so has Steve Hinton's family. He married Ed Maloney's daughter, Karen, and they have twins, Steve and Amanda. Maloney's youngest son, John, who is also an experienced pilot, works at Fighter Rebuilders as well. The crew has grown as their work has grown, and the atmosphere in the shop which is directly opposite the main hangar at Planes of Fame is busy. The telephone rings constantly and when I was there photographing the restoration of the P–38 the sound of riveting was incessant as work progressed on other projects.

Visitors are frequent at the museum and the caterer's truck comes early to keep the crew going until the 11:30 lunch break when they adjourn to their favorite Italian pizza parlor downtown. The shop mascot, "Browndog," is official greeter, receiving new visitors with appropriate suspicion, and old friends with excitement and enthusiasm. His usual perch is either on the ancient back seat from a GMC

Chino Airport, from John Hinton's Luscombe. The Planes of Fame complex including Fighter Rebuilders is located on the left upper center. Clearly visible is Runway 21 *across the top of the photo, which the P–38 used on its first test flight.*

A view of the crowded yard at Planes of Fame. Joltin' Josie, the P-38, is on the left while in front is the museum's B-25. On the right is an A-26 Invader and in the foreground are a Corsair and a Hellcat awaiting rebuilds. Tom Huston

Visitors to Planes of Fame can see this B-17 on static display close to the main entrance. Off to its left is a Lockheed Lodestar, and in the background is the remains of a B-50 bomber. Many of the Planes of Fame aircraft are used in movie work. At the time of this writing, Steve Hinton was working on Flight of the Intruder in Hawaii.

Suburban positioned next to Steve's desk or in the "cockpit" of the tug. In addition, Steve and Karen have twins and they are at the shop almost every day.

Having seen Steve Hinton fly John Sandberg's *Tsunami* at the Reno Air Races as well as the P–38

There are several Corsairs at Chino Airport. This dusty example with its wings folded is parked in front of Fighter Rebuilders.

A bird's-eye view of the 475th Fighter Group room at Planes of Fame in Chino, California. The 475th was one of the few all–P–38 fighter groups in the Pacific theater during World War II, and this mini-museum at Chino is dedicated to the Group. Its archives include memorabilia such as books, photographs and other items directly related to the history of the Group. Hanging from the ceiling is a large-scale radio-controlled model of a P–38. The room is occasionally open to visitors.

The yard at Planes of Fame is crowded with a variety of warbirds. In this view looking out the door of the shop, you can see the tail of a Corsair and behind it a Hellcat.

and other warbirds at Chino, I was interested in talking to him about his flying. I remarked that what impressed me most was his ability to easily and quickly go from one airplane to the next. With about 5,000 total hours in the air at this writing and 4,000 of them in warbirds, Hinton said: "Flying is flying; it's mostly headwork. I was checked out in the Mustang after 250 hours. Warbirds are not that difficult to fly. The physical pushing and pulling of the controls is not the same but it's not that difficult. However, you have to be current. Although there were a couple of warbirds that were difficult to fly, like the P–39, most of them are really not that difficult."

Watching Hinton at the controls of an airplane, it's obvious that he is a natural. He continued: "My favorite airplane is the Sabrejet. You have all that

Ed Maloney, founder of Planes of Fame, is the man who saw the value of saving all these aircraft many years ago. He founded the museum in 1960.

Steve Hinton, pilot and founder of Fighter Rebuilders.

Hinton with his wife Karen and children Steve and Amanda.

Twins Stephen and Amanda Hinton in their stroller in front of the P-38J. Port and starboard twins, Model 111 is Steve and 113 is Amanda.

power. You're sitting in a great cockpit that is air conditioned and comfortable. And my favorite propeller warbird is the Bearcat. There is just nothing like it." During my many visits to Chino, I have seen Hinton in at least a half-dozen different airplanes. The museum's B–25 is often used in air shows and on one of my first visits *Betty Grable*, as she is called, was loaded up with the crew from the shop to make a

In the cockpit of the Planes of Fame P-51, Hinton taxis up to the main gate at the rear of the museum. There is also a passenger in the back seat. The back seat accommodation in this particular airplane is good, and a passenger is able to either talk with the pilot or listen to the radio communications between plane and ground or with other planes. Ventilation is not great, however, but the ride makes up for any minor discomfort.

Hinton checking out the Planes of Fame P-51 prior to flight. The museum offers warbird rides in return for a contribution to their nonprofit organization.

Hinton in the cockpit of the Skyraider that was rebuilt immediately after the P-38 was finished. This airplane arrived at the shop in particularly rough shape.

A typical scene in the yard at Fighter Rebuilders. Steve Hinton and two volunteer helpers are working on preparing the museum's Messerschmitt 109 for flight. The Corsair in the background awaits its turn.

19

Some of the crew in the yard at Fighter Rebuilders. From left to right: John Hinton, Steve Hinton, Kevin Eldridge, Matt Nightingale, Bob Nightingale, Pat Nightingale, Joe Haley and Dennis Sanders. Haley, a commercial airline pilot, is restoring a Russian Yak which he plans to race at Reno, while Dennis Sanders, also in the restoration business, often flies a Sea Fury at Reno.

Kevin Eldridge, the hydraulic specialist at Fighter Rebuilders. Eldridge installed all of the hydraulic plumbing on the P–38 as well as working on the engine and other components as the need arose. He is a pilot and has more than 50 hours in the museum's Mustang. Eldridge has a bachelor's degree in finance, and intends to become an airline pilot.

Rich Palmer was one of the two Fighter Rebuilders mechanics to be permanently assigned to the P-38 project. Palmer is also a photographer and accomplished video camera operator, having produced a number of shows for Ed Maloney on the museum's collection of warbirds.

John Maloney is often seen behind the wheel of the museum's P-47. His work on the rebuild of the P-38 included a little bit of everything, but primarily sheet metal. Maloney is an extremely competent pilot and is seen annually at the Reno Air Races flying the Super Corsair.

fly-by at the Winter National Drag Races at Pomona, California.

Hinton's crew is dedicated to their boss; they are like an extended family. Rich Palmer, one of the mechanics assigned to the P-38 rebuild, has known Hinton since high school as did Kevin Eldridge, the hydraulic specialist. John Maloney, now Hinton's brother-in-law, does just about anything that comes his way in the shop. Maloney is also a pilot of some note and is seen annually at Reno flying the *Super Corsair* racer.

The rest of the crew includes John Hinton, Steve's younger brother, who mainly works on sheet metal. Alan Wojciak, another ace sheet metal man, also flies warbirds when he has the opportunity. Mike "Maj" McDougall primarily is responsible for

much of the painting done at the shop. He is also building up hours in some of the museum's airplanes. Jim Dale, or "JD," is an all-around mechanic who has his commercial ticket as well as his multi-engine license. Then there is Mike "Lefty" McGuckian who seemed to spend most of his time building the nose of the P-38. He is backed up by Matt Nightingale and Dennis Collins, who both did a little bit of everything on the restoration. John Kagihara, or "JK," was the other man assigned by Hinton to the P-38 rebuild. Kagihara is a licensed airframe mechanic, totally dedicated to warbirds, and knows the P-38 as well as anyone does.

In addition to the above regulars there are a considerable number of friends and volunteers who come by to help. The atmosphere at the shop is

John Hinton (Steve's younger brother), a sheet metal man at Fighter Rebuilders, poses in front of his 1949 Luscombe. Hinton put in many hours on the P-38, especially during the last part of the restoration and just before first flight.

Alan Wojciak working on the wing for John Sandberg's P-51 at Fighter Rebuilders.

Mike "Maj" McDougall, the resident painter at Fighter Rebuilders, in front of a Supermarine Spitfire that has just emerged from restoration after being freshly painted.

Jim "JD" Dale checking out a detail on the Skyraider that is undergoing a rebuild. Dale can do just about everything that comes along, including sheet metal and engine work. He is a pilot and holds his commercial ticket as well as multi-engine rating.

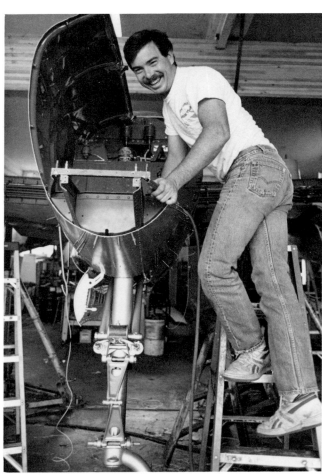

Mike "Lefty" McGuckian was a sheet metal expert at Fighter Rebuilders. Born in Redlands, California, McGuckian has been a lifelong airplane enthusiast who, in the beginning, came to Planes of Fame as a volunteer. He was soon on the payroll at Fighters and during the course of the P-38 rebuild fabricated three separate Lightning noses, one for Stephen Grey's airplane, one for a Confederate Air Force ship and one for Josie. He has since started his own restoration shop at Chino Airport.

Matt Nightingale, one of the younger employees at Fighter Rebuilders, worked on a variety of P-38 components during the rebuild. He is also a pilot with more than 100 hours and is studying aeronautical science at night school.

John Kagihara, known as "JK," at work in the cockpit of the P-38. Kagihara is a licensed airframe mechanic, as are most of the full-time people at Fighter Rebuilders. Born in Hawaii, he moved to California at a young age, attended schools there and has been with Steve Hinton for more than two years. His love for warbirds extends to making amazingly beautiful scale models as well.

warm and friendly, and there is always something interesting going on. For warbird and aviation enthusiasts, that small corner of the Chino airport is a magnet.

Backing up Fighter Rebuilders for engine work is JRS Enterprises in Minneapolis, Minnesota. JRS does all of Steve Hinton's major engine work on the warbird powerplants. The company is owned by John Sandberg, who sponsors the racer *Tsunami*. Hinton is building a P-51 for Sandberg.

Fighter Rebuilders' mascot, Browndog, sits in one of his favorite places. If it moves, he wants to ride on it. A lot of the nights he spends at the airport, but sometimes John Maloney, John Hinton, and Maj take him home with them. They all room together.

Bob Pond, co-owner of Joltin' Josie, *often visited Planes of Fame and Fighter Rebuilders during the restoration process. Here, he is preparing to go up in Josie. Pond is a former Navy pilot with an extensive collection not only of* warbirds but other types of aircraft as well. His Planes of Fame East is located outside of Minneapolis, Minnesota, at Flying Cloud Airport. The P–38 spends half the year there and half the year at Chino.

Steve Hinton and a Planes of Fame volunteer, Mark DeLaurell, work on the landing gear of the museum's Messerschmitt 109. The picture was taken on a Saturday, a particularly busy day at Planes of Fame due to the fact that many volunteers are on hand, eager to learn more about the collection and to actually help Hinton and his crew work on the airplanes.

The refinished main spar on Stephen Grey's P–38. In the background is the dual-control Mustang, a one-of-a-kind project that took shape at the same time as the P–38.

Hinton poses in front of the museum's Griffon-powered Mk 19 Spitfire.

26

Steve Hinton and Dave Morris, one of the crew at Fighter Rebuilders, discuss a detail concerning the Spitfire's rebuild.

Some people have pictures of their girlfriend or their baby in their wallet, others carry pictures of their favorite airplanes. A close-up of a wallet of a Planes of Fame volunteer.

Chapter 2

Lockheed and Its Lightning

In July of 1938 work began at the Lockheed Corporation in Burbank, California, on the prototype XP–38. The Army Air Corps had finally given Lockheed the go-ahead to build a plane that would write one of the most fascinating chapters in military aviation history. Maj. Ben Kelsey began a series of flight tests in January of 1939 which culminated in a spectacular cross-country flight on February 11. He was welcomed at Wright Field in Ohio by Gen. Henry H. "Hap" Arnold, chief of the Army Airs Corps, who urged Kelsey to fly the plane on to Mitchell Field just outside New York City essentially to make a

The airplane rolling out of the Lockheed test shed is the second prototype P–38 that pilot Ben Kelsey flew across the country early in 1939 to demonstrate to the Army Air Corps generals the machine's high-performance capabilities. Unfortunately, the plane crashed on landing at the end of the cross-country dash but nevertheless, the Army liked what they saw and further development aircraft were promptly ordered. The prototype aircraft were all highly polished. Note the dummy machine guns and the movie camera operator documenting the rollout. Photographer Erik Miller saw this picture in the National Geographic and was so excited about the airplane, he decided then and there he was going to work for Lockheed. Lockheed

splash in the daily newspapers. The Air Force felt the need for some exciting publicity and the new airplane gave plenty of evidence that it was going to be a success.

Kelsey chose to continue on to New York but unfortunately as he came in to land, a combination of problems arose that he was unable to deal with and he crash-landed just short of the runway. Kelsey walked away, but the prototype P–38 was a write-off. Despite this inauspicious debut, the Air Force was so pleased with the performance of the airplane that a contract to Lockheed was quickly drawn up. Within two months they were authorized to build thirteen so-called "service test" aircraft. These were known as YP–38s and the first one flew in September of 1940. The last one was delivered in the spring of the following year. According to Jeff Ethell, an expert on the P–38, only 196 production P–38s were built in 1941, not including the YP aircraft. By then the United States Army Air Corps not only wanted the plane, but there were also orders from France and

Lockheed test pilot "Nick" Nicholson in the cockpit of a test aircraft. He is wearing heavy winter gear to protect himself from the cold during high-altitude testing. Erik Miller

A P–38 prototype taxis past a line-up of Hudson bombers destined for England. Lockheed

Tony LeVier

As I began research for this book everyone I talked to asked if I had spoken with Tony LeVier—"Mr. P-38," someone called him. He is recognized as the living P-38 expert and still works for Lockheed, now as a consultant on safety issues. For ten years he was chief experimental test pilot (1945–1955). In his career he has flown virtually every Lockheed airplane, including jets. I asked him what it took for a test pilot to become number one as he did. LeVier responded: "I was suspicious of everything, always suspicious of the hardware and I was a stickler for detail. In the cockpit I got rid of sharp edges on the controls and I changed the way the stick grip rotated so that it felt more natural. Today they call all that 'ergonomics.' And I was also an inventor. I invented the master caution warning light. I developed the hot mike and I invented the automatic stores release. That's a device that if you accidentally lose a bomb or a tank off of one side of the airplane, the other side can go too. That way the airplane stays balanced. And I put the trim switch on the stick."

LeVier sits at a desk surrounded by photographs of the Lockheed airplanes that he has flown, and some he hasn't, like the SR-71. He loves to talk about his life's work and most of all about the Lockheed Lightning, the P-38:

"Here was an airplane that was totally new and for 1939 when it first flew was absolutely revolutionary. It had flying characteristics unlike any other airplane up to that time. To begin with, it had counterrotating propellers which really made the airplane. Kelly Johnson, Lockheed's chief designer at the time, was given credit for it although all airplanes have lots of people involved in creating them. It was decided we were going to have two engines, side by side, with a center pod to hold the pilot and the nose of the airplane with the guns and ammo. We'd have twin booms on it to a rear tail spanning across with dual rudders.

"It was an absolute breeze to fly. There is nothing easier to taxi than an airplane with tricycle landing gear. We did not have a steerable nose wheel but if you didn't taxi too fast you could turn it easily, left brake, left rudder, and it turns. On takeoff it was easy. There was no torque—thanks to the counterrotating props and all you had to do was to get it to a certain speed and the airplane would just fly off.

"If you had it trimmed right, it would just fly off. The minimum control speed of the P-38 in those days we determined to be 120 mph indicated. Then, if you lost an engine you could hold all the power that you had on the other engine if it was wide open. A lot of times, people who lost an engine on takeoff wouldn't have enough speed and maybe

they weren't even situated right in the cockpit to be able to get full left or right rudder and I learned early on the way to do it. I'd get in there and adjust the pedals. I'd get my seat where I wanted it and adjust the pedals so that I could jam left or right rudder stiff-legged if I needed it."

One of the major initial problems that a few of the Lockheed test pilots encountered during the Lightning's early development work was the phenomenon of compressibility which rears its ugly head with certain airplanes in a high-speed dive. Not unlike a huge wall of water, the wall of air building up in front of the diving airplane makes it extremely difficult for the pilot to pull out of the dive. Instead, the airplane tends to want to tuck or to increase the dive angle to a point where recovery is impossible. I asked Tony LeVier about his experiences with compressibility while testing early models of the P-38 Lightning:

"I was over what is now Edwards Air Force Base at the time near Muroc Dry Lake on a test flight in the early 1940s when I made the final dive of the day with this P-38 that had dive flaps installed, which we hoped would help deal with this compressibility or 'tuck' problem. I made the dive from 35,000 feet, almost straight down, actually it was sixty degrees. We found that to be the optimum, pushing over from 35,000 and at about 32,000 the airplane started to tuck. This added five degrees over the previous dive by Milo Burcham, the other test pilot, and now it had a very severe tuck but I was able to hold the angle and I rode it down to 20,000 feet where we normally started our pull-out. And I started pulling to try to get it out of this dive. At 19,000 feet I had only gained one degree. The next thousand I pushed a couple more degrees and pretty soon I was at about 10,000 feet. That was a very gamey thing because I'm eating up altitude like 800 or 900 feet per second and only a few seconds from the ground out over Edwards, pulling like crazy to get this thing out of the dive. I had a battery of red lights here in front of my nose and these were all primary stress points on the airplane, both wing and boom bending as well as the stabilizer and critical places like that. All six lights came on. They would come on if I exceeded design limit loads on those critical parts. But I managed to recover and flew it slowly home to Burbank. It turned out that the airplane had been beefed up at those critical places but nevertheless I had reached the design limt of the airplane."

Tony LeVier was lucky compared to what happened to his colleague, test pilot Ralph Verdon. LeVier related the story:

"Well, it didn't always work out so successfully, I remember back in 1941 or 1942, when I was not yet in engineering and we were watching a test dive

Lockheed test pilot Tony LeVier poses for the company photographer Erik Miller on the wing of a later model P–38, possibly a P–38J. Miller often flew with LeVier and said, "He had a touch that was phenomenal. He was an expert at formation flying and he and Milo Burcham could put a wing tip into the window of the camera plane and keep it there if you asked him to." Erik Miller

by Ralph Verdon, 'Killer' Verdon he was called. He was a husky ex-wrestler and had been a United Airlines captain before he joined Lockheed. He was diving this airplane and in this particular test was to dive with a spring tab on the elevator which was thought to be maybe necessary to help pull out of these dives and at the conclusion of the dive he was going to come down across the original factory, factory B in Burbank, at high speed to show the brass who were out from Washington. At that period of time, the P–38 was the fastest thing in the country and whenever you saw one it was going fast, just going like hell all of the time. We heard him coming. It was loud. Nothing like it. And we heard suddenly a kind of bang and both engines were going at full rpm and clearly something terrible had happened. In fact, he had pulled the tail off and the airplane flipped upside down and went into an inverted spin. Then came an awful thud. You could almost feel it when he hit the ground and he was killed."

LeVier went on to tell more about the P–38's history:

"Now as far as maneuverability, the P–38 did not maneuver as well as it should have to be a fighter but it was primarily designed to be an interceptor—to climb up to high altitudes quickly and shoot down a bomber. But pretty soon the war came along and we're building these airplanes by the hundreds and they want to use it for everything. They want to use it for fighter-bomber escorts, to take on other fighters, and to do photo reconnaissance. It did a great job there because with the turbocharged engines it could climb high and fast but it didn't have any guns in that configuration and so the pilots didn't have any means to protect themselves.

"The other thing about the P–38 was that it had a beautiful stall, a normal 1g stall. No airplane had a better one. It didn't roll or snap one way or the other. I used to stall it, for example, with one engine down. Stall it right on the deck to demonstrate to other pilots, 'hey, this airplane is manageable.'

"I remember my first flight in the 38. I got checked out by accident because I was low on the seniority list and the old-timers knew this and they didn't want these young kids flying it before they did and so they came up with a ruling that said they'll check them out in terms of seniority. Well, that isn't the way it should have been done at all. They should have selected the pilots that they thought had the qualifications.

"Well, one day over at the pilot house before I was in engineering in early 1942, it was at the end of the day and they called in a last-minute test and nobody wanted it. They wanted to go home and they knew they would be stuck there for another hour and a half, and John Meyers, who was one of our pilots and a helluva nice guy, said, 'Let's check LeVier out.' Just like that, and everybody said, 'Yeah, that's a good idea.'

"So they put me in this airplane and one of the pilots went out to check me out. His name was Bill Mundy and he showed me how to start it. Well, I knew how to do all that stuff but I hadn't had anything at all to do with the airplane yet. So I got it fired up and I took off. Now, I hadn't studied the airplane at all and I didn't feel too comfortable and to be perfectly honest if I'd had my choice I probably wouldn't have done it but here was my opportunity and everybody was watching. Well, I did okay. The airplane turned out to be a breeze to fly but it was strange to me. I don't like things like that. I want to know what the hell I'm doing. But I ran off the things on the list and came down and landed okay and it was a breeze. I still didn't know the airplane. I didn't know the systems so I took the handbook home that night and I read that thing from cover to cover. The next day I was here, back at work, first one, and they put my name at the head of the list. I got the first airplane that came out and it turned out to be a great flight. I knew more. I was ready."

England. The Air Corps had ordered 673 aircraft by September of 1940.

Not counting the XPs and YPs, sixty-eight airplanes had been built by the fall of 1941. These were P–38Es and, according to Ethell, 210 of them were built up until April 1942 when the F model came on the line. This was the first P–38 model to see combat.

Then came the P–38G and P–38H with more powerful Allisons incorporating turbochargers. The J model P–38 was the version that finally incorporated the many design elements that were to make the plane such a fantastic warbird. Nearly 3,000 Js were built, but the final 210 that came off the line were the only ones that included such amenities as dive brakes, aileron boost and even improved heating for the cockpit.

Just short of 10,000 P–38s were built by the end of the war in 1945. Many of these were special aircraft designed for photo reconnaissance or for

A factory shot of the early P–38 production line before it became mechanized. The center section of the airplane was picked up by a crane and dropped into position to be worked on. The finished airplane was taken out the doors at the top of the photo. Landing gear was installed and the plane rolled forward. Lockheed

The Burbank Lockheed factory in the early 1940s. Lodestars are off in the left corner with British markings. Since there is no evidence of turbochargers being fitted to the P–38s in the picture, these planes may be part of the batch that was ordered by Great Britain.

The Lockheed factory P-38 assembly line in 1941 or early 1942. This Lightning is probably an H model, indicated by the smaller air intakes in the engine cowling. Note the great amount of handwork that was used to build these early planes. Lockheed

The business end of a P-38 on the test-firing range. Ammunition cans are at either side. Erik Miller said that the powerful machine guns and 20 mm cannon quickly wore away the sand that filled the bullet-stop. They were forever replenishing the sand. Erik Miller

Later in the war. The P-38J models are on the assembly lines and the activity level is obviously much higher than in earlier photographs of the same area. An Allison engine is moving through space above the busy assembly area. Lockheed

Large air view of the Burbank factory: this is a view looking east, and the Lockheed factory is in the upper area of the photo. During the war a huge expanse of camouflage netting was laid out over the factory. It was strung between tall 14x14 foot posts that were 60 feet high. They were done up with guy wires and tied to each other. Then rolls and rolls of chicken wire were laid out. The wire was then sprayed with adhesive which was covered with chicken feathers and then painted to look like a village with houses, streets and lawns. The whole thing had been drawn up in a nearby movie studio and then set up to cover the factory from enemy eyes in the sky. Lockheed

Wartime security was tight—even on the Van Nuys firing range. The tape below the guns covers the plane numbers; Lockheed did not want the Japanese to know how many airplanes they had made. And a security guard stands watch in the cockpit. Note the canvas bag for collecting the empty cartridges. Erik Miller

The P–38M night fighter version had a raised seat behind the pilot for the radar operator. The viewer for the scope sits directly in front of the operator's face. This Lockheed photo clearly shows the redesigned bubble canopy which apparently was hinged on the trailing edge as was the pilot's canopy. Note the rearview mirror for the pilot just above his windshield, and the scuffed and chipped black paint. The P–38M was not a great success due to the fact that the P–61 Black Widow was already in service when it began testing. Lockheed

A P–38's guns being test-fired on the firing range during the night. Test-firing was carried out extensively near the factory during the war, until the neighbors complained and Lockheed was forced to move the firing range to Van Nuys, California. Lockheed

One of the last and most interesting versions of the Lightning was the P–38M night fighter. In his book Fighting Lightnings, *Michael O'Leary reported that flight testing of the P–38M did not begin until July of 1945, and even though testing revealed that it had better performance than the P–61 Black Widow, the latter airplane was already in service and doing an excellent job against the enemy. An order of 75 M models was commissioned by the Air Force. The radar was fitted under the nose in a fiberglass pod while the radar operator sat behind the pilot under a bubble canopy in a raised seat, with the radar scope itself directly in front of his face.* Erik Miller

other kinds of missions. But the P–38 made its name in the skies over the Pacific. The harsh European climate was one of the principal factors that caused it not to be one of the most favorite aircraft by American pilots, however. Also, it was still suffering from teething troubles, and men like Tony LeVier spent countless hours in Europe as tech reps trying to sort out problems as they arose.

Erik Miller

Erik Miller was a photographer for Lockheed Aircraft Company for thirty-one years beginning in March of 1941. He did much of his air-to-air photography using a 5x7 in. Fairchild aerial camera, and then a Speed Graphic (4x5 in.). Oftentimes he would use a military aerial camera that was electrically operated and had 4x5 in. roll film installed, making probably twenty exposures while in the air, a lot for that period in time. Many of the flights that he went up on were not designed for a photo shoot. He would often be supercargo on a test plane. Today, his photographs are a large part of the Lockheed photo archives in Burbank.

Miller was one of a large number of Lockheed photographers, most of whom were shooting nuts and bolts type photography. But he found himself doing a great deal of air-to-air work as well. He worked hard at setting up the planes with attractive backgrounds, such as Mount Baldy, or with interesting cloud formations. Going up in any handy Hudson bomber or a Lockheed Lodestar, even a B–17, Miller would hang out an open window and shoot his pictures, using to a large degree "good old sheet Kodachrome" as he said, as well as a variety of black and white pan films. Exposures were usually made at 1/125 or 1/250 of a second. Altitude for picture
Continued on next page

taking was not that high, since he wanted to incorporate the mountains for a backdrop in many of his shots. Burbank was a busy place during the war. Not only were P–38s rolling off the assembly lines, but Hudson bombers and even B–17s were also being built by Lockheed.

There were two groups of pilots then, the production pilots and the test pilots. Production pilots flew the squawks off the airplanes as they came off the assembly lines while the test pilots like LeVier did the experimental work—"the dirty work," as Miller called it.

There were over a hundred production pilots at one time and with a P–38 coming off the line at the rate of one per hour, the sky was full of airplanes being put through their paces.

Miller said, "I had the best job at Lockheed."

With a top security clearance he got into all sorts of secret places (excluding the famous Skunk Works). He often went up in P–38s and spoke in glowing terms of a well-known Lockheed pilot named Clarence "Soupy" Shoup, who was an acceptance pilot. Miller tells of one particular piggyback flight with Shoup—just "for a lark," sitting in the back, on the wing beam, bent forward in an uncomfortable posture, taking the place of all the radio gear that normally sits on the wing beam.

As Miller recalled: "I accidentally hit the toggle switch for the replacement radio, turning it off so that we couldn't reach the tower, and our short fifteen-minute flight lasted an hour and a half. But it was great, and what impressed me most was the stability of the airplane—the solidness of it. It was just like a fortress. It was rigid and extremely sensi-

One of Erik Miller's first air-to-air photos taken for Lockheed, a publicity photo that was used by Lockheed to recruit workers for the assembly lines. Apparently this sort of image was very effective in recruitment, because Miller reported that all kinds of people were on the lines building airplanes. Even Marilyn Monroe was supposed to have worked on the P–38 assembly line for a while. Preachers, judges, band leaders, all kinds of people worked there. Erik Miller

A group of P–38s over the Pacific Ocean. Miller took this photo from the open belly door on a Hudson bomber. Erik Miller

tive to power. You could feel yourself being pushed back when the pilot applied the power to the engines. It was just like being on a track."

Miller remembers how the Lockheed bureaucrats gradually produced more paperwork and forms that had to be filled out before each flight. "I couldn't wait that long," he said. "The weather would change too fast and there wasn't time to make out a request. Soupy loved to go flying and loved to do the photo shoots and I would just walk into his office and say 'do you want to go flying' and he'd say 'sure'—he had enough authority to just go and grab an airplane and I had hundreds of flights on that basis."

A P–38 over the South Pacific. Note the ships below. Col.
Charles MacDonald

Chapter 3

The Lightning Goes to War

Oddly enough, the British gave the P–38 its name. They had ordered several hundred P–38s early on in the war and dubbed the model "Lightning," but they were disappointed in the airplane's performance. Production problems in the United States had forced Lockheed to deliver the airplanes to the British without turbochargers, and they abruptly canceled the order. However, the name stuck and as production slowly caught up with the needs of the US Army Air Corps, Lightnings were soon in the hands of pilots who were impatient to get them into the air.

While many planes of the first production remained in the United States as training and development aircraft, by 1942 the first P–38s finally saw combat, five years after its inception. The first batch were sent to Australia, in the photo-recon version, the F–4. In June of 1942, P–38Es were in service in the Aleutian campaign but this theater proved to be an inauspicious start. The weather in the Aleutian Islands was fearful, with fog the order of the day during most of the year. Without adequate radar and other navigation aids which came later, the P–38 pilots suffered terrible attrition mainly due to not being able to find their way home from a mission.

By mid 1942, P–38s were being ferried to England in groups of fours, always led by a B–17

A group of early P–38s in flight over southern California in 1942. These were undoubtedly training planes, as indicated by the numbers on the nose.

equipped with adequate navigation gear, and slowly a stockpile of P–38s was amassed for the newly-formed Eighth Air Force Fighter Command. The first kill for the airplane was made off of Iceland by Lt. Elza Shahan of the 27th Fighter Squadron. He happened upon a Focke-Wulf Condor twin-engine plane that was known to shadow Allied convoys. In company with a P–40 from the same squadron he jumped the Fw and quickly sent it into a spiraling dive into the North Atlantic. Not only was this the first kill for a P–38, but it was also the first enemy plane to be shot down by a USAAF pilot in the European theater.

As Jeff Ethell points out in his splendid history *P–38 Lightning* (Zokeisha/Crown), the airplane was the only high-altitude fighter that the United States had in its inventory and we wasted no time in putting the aircraft through its paces. The North African campaign was the first real test of the P–38, its debut for the Luftwaffe.

Shepherding bombers and strafing troops and armored columns in the middle of the desert, the P–38 has been given tremendous credit by historians for helping turn the tide against the Germans and the Italians. By 1943, the German Air Force had suffered severe losses at the hands of American P–38 pilots who found the airplane to be not only fast and maneuverable but also an impressive weapons platform.

In his book, Ethell quotes Johannes Steinhoff, the famous Luftwaffe ace: "I had encountered the long range P–38 Lightning fighter during the last few days of the North African campaign. Our opinion of this twin-boomed, twin-engined aircraft was divided. Our old Messerschmitts were still, perhaps, a little faster. But pilots who had fought them said that the Lightnings were capable of appreciably tighter turns and that they would be on your tail before you knew what was happening. The machine guns mounted in the nose supposedly produced a concentration of fire from which there was no escape. Certainly the effect was reminiscent of a watering can when one of those dangerous apparitions started firing tracer, and it was essential to prevent them maneuvering into a position from which they could bring their guns to bear."

The P–38 met with less enthusiasm in the European theater, however. One of the principal

A lone P–38 in company with a B–17 Flying Fortress flight at high altitude.

reasons for this was the simple fact that the cockpit heater was inadequate to deal with the cold temperatures found at high altitudes over Europe. Pilots were suffering from the cold and found themselves in no condition to do battle with the Luftwaffe if their windshields were frosted over or if their bodies were so stiff from the cold that they couldn't adequately respond to the demands of a dogfight.

There were problems with the Allisons as well, and engine failures in those early days were frequent. Test pilots from Lockheed were sent to England to try to help sort out some of the problems. Tony LeVier spent weeks in England and Northern Ireland in a crash program to attempt to find some solutions. But by the time they thought they had it sorted out, Gen. Jimmy Doolittle had signed the order to replace the P-38 with the P-51, and the Lightning was phased out of Eighth Air Force service.

Nevertheless, the P-38 had given a great account of itself in North Africa and in the Mediterranean theater. One pilot, I. Newton Perry, now living in Santa Barbara, California, was flying pathfinder missions out of Bari, Italy. He and his fellow pilot, Greg Milne, once flew a six hour and fifty minute mission to Berlin and back in their P-38s. Both pilots have nothing but great things to say about the airplane. Perry, a musician by trade, was a careful, serious pilot who never saw a single enemy aircraft during his whole tour while flying photo missions

out of Bari. He and Milne led flights of B-24s and B-17s to the targets in Germany, showing them the best routes to avoid heavy weather and clouds, making it easier for the large formations to maintain their protective formation without crashing into each other. They were attached to the 154th Weather Reconnaissance Squadron from the Fifteenth Air Force Headquarters. The P-38s that they flew were known as pathfinders and had a nose extension fitted that allowed a navigator and a radar set to be in the nose to precisely guide the bombers to the

With their pathfinder P-38 fueled up and ready to go, lead pilot I. Newton Perry and his navigator Gordon Hackbarth prepare for their longest mission, a seven-hour run to Berlin and back from Bari, Italy. On the left is another pilot, Greg Milne, a good friend of Perry's who flew a second Lightning on this long mission. Attached to the 15th Fighter Command, these P-38s acted as guides for the B-17s and B-24s that were blasting Germany's cities unmercifully by mid 1945. The navigator sat in the nose with his radar, watching for cloud cover, and Perry, the pilot, would relay the information via code to the bombers. Perry, today a musician and orchestra leader in Santa Barbara, California, loved the P-38 and emphasized how easy it was to fly: "Once you had the trim established and set the way you wanted it, you felt like you could sit back and read the Reader's Digest all the way to Berlin and back. It was a very quiet airplane compared to the P-51 and a dream to fly, in large part, thanks to the counter-rotating propellers." Stars & Stripes

Lt. I. Newton Perry with his P-38 Oh Pardon Me, used for photo reconnaissance out of Bari, Italy. I. Newton Perry

target while avoiding cloud cover. They also flew a so-called droop snoot from time to time, which had a bombardier and a bomb sight fitted. The droop snoot led an entire pack of P–38s equipped with a heavy bomb load, and when the lead P–38 droop snoot gave the command everyone behind dropped their bombs.

It is interesting to note that by June 1944 pilots Milne and Perry had been issued electric flight suits that could be plugged into the electrical system of the airplane, and by means of a rheostat, turn up the heat in what was somewhat like a great electric blanket. With cockpit temperatures indicating minus fifty and minus sixty degrees, an electrically heated suit was a great asset, to say the least.

Electrically heated flying suits were not required for the South Pacific, however, and the P–38 was without question the star of the show in the war

This photo was taken by John Phillips, a Life *war correspondent, on the island of Sardinia in July of 1944. Antoine de Saint-Exupery, the famous French aviator and writer, is preparing to depart on a flight from which he never returned. The plane is the photo reconnaissance version of the P–38 known as the F–5B. Saint-Exupery's airplane carries French markings, but he was attached to the 23rd Photo Recon Wing of the Mediterranean Allied Tactical Air Force under General Eaker. Note the drop tanks under the main spar as well as the numerous missions painted on the nose. The opening in the side of the nose is for an aerial camera. The wheel chocks have been removed from the port side, while the starboard wheel still has not been cleared. The officer in the foreground is motioning the pilot to back off the throttle so that the recalcitrant wheel chock can be removed. Also, the rearview mirror has been affixed to the top of the windshield. Rear vision on the P–38 was never great and was one of the few complaints that pilots had about the airplane. John Phillips*

against the Japanese. Initially, the Lightning was used in its photo reconnaissance configuration, operating out of Australia in April of 1942. By August of that year, at least thirty fighter P–38s were being off-loaded in Australia and were soon headed to the front. It was John Mitchell of the 339th Fighter Squadron who is given credit for first taking over a number of P–38s and putting them through their paces against the enemy. Mitchell was to later lead the famous Yamamoto mission that shot down the Japanese commander in chief in the Solomon Islands.

To get a better feel for what it was like to fly the P–38 in the Pacific theater, I interviewed several well-known Lightning pilots. The first man I spoke with was Col. Charles H. MacDonald, whose P–38 *Putt Putt Maru* is a legendary machine among warbird enthusiasts.

Col. Charles H. MacDonald

The Florida panhandle is flat and featureless and the Interstate cuts across its midsection like a knife. I had flown into Mobile, Alabama, the closest airport to a small town called Defuniak Springs, to pay a call on Col. Charles H. MacDonald, US Air Force, retiree. Colonel Mac, as he is known to his friends, was commanding officer of the 475th Fighter Group, an all-P–38 unit of General Kenney's Fifth Air Force. MacDonald is the highest-ranking, living ace from the Pacific theater with twenty-seven confirmed kills to his credit in his P–38, the famed *Putt Putt Maru*. He is the fifth highest ranking ace in the US Air Force and the seventh overall of American aces. With the help of Pete Madison, also of the 475th, I arranged to meet with Mac at, appropriately enough, the local McDonald's restaurant. He figured he would have to lead me to his home which is out in the countryside, northwest of town and hard for a stranger to find. Sure enough, within ten minutes he and his dog turned up in the pickup and after a few welcoming words, the retired Air Force ace guided me to his home in the jungles of Florida.

After about fifteen minutes of driving we turned off onto a bumpy, high-crowned dirt road that took us to his property. The sign on the gate read, "Wild Life Preserve—No Hunting" and as we approached his house I noticed a fenced-in, screened-over cage-like structure that was home for a family of ducks. Off in the distance was a large pond that also had a structure adjacent to it. "That's where I go in the evening with a drink in my hand to watch the wild life," said MacDonald.

The scene was rural and peaceful, a fitting place for a retired Air Force colonel after a lengthy

Col. Charles H. MacDonald, former commanding officer of the 475th Fighter Group (an all–P–38 outfit) relaxes on his porch in Defuniak Springs, Florida, with his two dogs, Bear and Busch. MacDonald retired from the Air Force in 1961 and is the highest-ranking living ace from the Pacific theater, with 27 confirmed kills.

and full military career. He had gone into the Army Air Corps in 1938 and won his wings the following year. On December 7, 1941, Mac found himself with a P–40 squadron at Pearl Harbor: "We were scrambled in the afternoon after they had all gone. I was at Wheeler Field and we were airborne in time to become targets for all the hysterical people on the ground. The hysteria was incredible. All the radio stations were broadcasting rumors that the Japanese were landing here, or the Japanese were landing there. Then we scrambled again during the night and you can imagine what it was like flying around in the middle of the night above Pearl Harbor without any lights. It was totally chaotic."

Colonel MacDonald was soon out of the P–40s and after Pearl harbor returned to the States to command a P–47 Fighter Group. By 1943, however, he found himself back in action and once more in the Pacific after his orders had been changed from a European theater destination. Oct. 15, 1943 was his baptism of fire in the cockpit of a P–38. Now executive officer with the 475th Fighter Group, he and one of his fellow officers, Lieutenant Ivey, went off into the air with two P-38s appropriated from the 433rd Squadron. They jumped enemy planes over the ocean near a place called Oro Bay in the Port Moresby area of New Guinea. The two pilots shot down four Japanese bombers and had two probables in just that one day.

MacDonald recalled: "Really, the P-38 was an extension of the human body. It was a wonderful airplane. The props counterrotated so there was never any torque problem and it did not have any

peculiarities to speak of. It was a very docile aircraft to fly and would do whatever you asked it to do and it performed beautifully. It would out-turn and out-climb the P-47; it had a great high-altitude capability with the turbochargers, and the airplane was strong.

"My most memorable experience was getting shot up very badly, having one engine out. The electrical systems were shot out so the prop on the good engine went into full rpm and I couldn't feather the prop on the other one, so it was touch and go. I was thirty miles out to sea but I got back. I thought if I could get high enough I would bail out, but I couldn't climb because the engine that was still working was overheating. All the coolant had been shot out and with my hydraulics out, I couldn't lower the gear so I bellied it in on the strip. She was full of holes and nothing was working except that one engine, and it had overheated to the point where it should have quit but it didn't. I had been concentrating on shooting down a Japanese bomber and a Zero came up behind me. I didn't see him. He was right between my tail booms when he let go."

I asked Mac how close he got to ensure a kill. "The closer the better," Mac said. "We were bore-sighted for a thousand feet so that within that range you had a good chance of getting a good hit. Of course you could get closer, the closer the better. When you start getting his pieces hitting you then you know you are too close. Or, as it happened to me once in the Philippines the Jap's engine oil came back and went all over the windshield and I couldn't see where the hell I was going. That is real discon-

A photo of Colonel MacDonald after only eight kills, as indicated on the side of the airplane. 475th Fighter Group archive

Colonel MacDonald poses for the 475th photographer in front of his P-38 Putt Putt Maru *with Generals Wurtsmith and Shulgren. Brig. Gen. Wurtsmith (whose nickname was "Squeeze" according to MacDonald) was head of the 5th Fighter Command. The picture was probably taken in the Philippines toward the end of the war. The P-38 shown here was the third P-38 (a J model) that MacDonald flew in the Pacific named* Putt Putt Maru. *Dennis Glen Cooper*

Colonel MacDonald with Col. Charles A. Lindbergh in front of Putt Putt Maru *on Hollandia, New Guinea. Col. Charles MacDonald*

certing. Engine oil is pretty damn sticky and it doesn't blow off."

MacDonald had the good fortune to work with Col. Charles A. Lindbergh who was attached to the 475th Fighter Group for a while. Serving as an advisor to the Army Air Corps, Lindbergh made a major contribution to the war effort by demonstrating to the pilots how they could extend the range of the P–38s by cutting rpm but maintaining a relatively high manifold pressure. Lindbergh became a good friend of the men of the 475th.

Modesty seems to be a quality often found in premier pilots. Colonel MacDonald is no different, and talks willingly but quietly about his war service. He received six Distinguished Flying Crosses, two Distinguished Service Crosses (this is next in line to the Congressional Medal of Honor), two Silver Stars, eleven Air Medals and the Legion of Merit.

When I asked MacDonald why the P–38 was so successful, he responded, "Because it was a natural for the Pacific theater. It had the range that the P–47 did not have. It was a helluva gun platform and most of all it had two engines. A lot of us made it home on just one engine. That airplane made us the heroes."

Pete Madison

H. N. "Pete" Madison is Chairman of the Board of Color Graphics Inc., a large and successful printing firm in Los Angeles. He also chairs the advisory board of the Planes of Fame Air Museum at Chino, and as a former member of the 475th Fighter Group is in charge of the room that is a tribute to the 475th. The room houses memorabilia including photographs, flight gear and models of P–38s, all of which pertain to the 475th Fighter Group.

Pete Madison flew 106 missions in P–38s under the helm of Colonel MacDonald in the South Pacific. When I interviewed him in his Los Angeles office, he had this to say:

"All of us had dramatic moments, almost on a daily basis out there, but I remember one particular incident that as I look back on it, testifies to the incredible strength and integrity of the P–38 airplane.

"I was on a strafing mission out of Hollandia [New Guinea]. Major McGuire was leading a group of about twelve of us. Our target was Manokwari on the western tip of New Guinea. It was a large and very strong Japanese base not like Rabaul, but still pretty big and we were pounding it hard. In fact, the base at Manokwari which we were trying to hit from Hollandia, had been by-passed, even by the Japanese on resupply, and our intelligence told us that they were in such bad straits for food that it was not a

Posing for the photographer, personnel of the 475th Fighter Group, Hollandia, New Guinea. Dennis Glen Cooper

The 475th Fighter Group parking area, Hollandia. Dennis Glen Cooper

good idea to get shot down in that area. Rumor was that the Japanese were not adverse to cannibalism.

"We were trying out a new technique that Col. Charles Lindbergh had been teaching us and that was how to use less fuel on our long overwater sorties. We would decrease our rpm, but keep up the manifold pressure, which meant an rpm as low as 1600 rpm. Well, this was a long strike and we still had our external tanks on as McGuire ordered us in to strafe the ships in the Manokwari harbor. I remember him specifically saying, 'Don't drop your tanks.'

"So, we began our run in and as I made my pass I could see my shells doing a job on the ships in the harbor. As I started to pull up I had a problem because I didn't have the recovery factor to gain altitude and believe it or not I mushed right into the forward mast of a Japanese freighter and it hit the mast with my right engine.

45

"This probably would not have happened if I had had a different rpm and manifold pressure setting, but I was only nineteen at the time and new boy in the Group. The impact flipped my airplane over on its back! Well, I immediately managed to right the airplane and started to make a gradual turn but I'm slipping down towards the water and suddenly the right propeller came off and went through the cockpit canopy and then back to the right vertical stabilizer, knocking it off. I was scared to death. I was bleeding. My instruments were all running wild and I was in shock.

"At that moment, Hal Gray and Jim Mooring flew alongside of me, and got my attention, as my radios were out. I looked over and saw Hal drop his tanks. Suddenly it hit me. I hadn't yet dropped my

The unsung heroes, the crew chiefs who kept the P–38s flying. Here is S.Sgt. D. C. Todd with his plane, in the South Pacific. Lockheed

46

Peeling off for landing, 475th Fighter Group. Dennis Glen Cooper

P–38s returning from a mission doing a flyby over the strip. Dennis Glen Cooper

tanks which I should have done as soon as I righted the airplane. So I dropped them and I was then able to maintain altitude and even climb a bit and turn back towards our base at Hollandia, holding about 160 mph indicated, on one engine, bleeding, a hole in the canopy, with those guys escorting me home.

"But it wasn't so simple because I couldn't get any more power and any more altitude as I was close to stalling a number of times. The next problem was fuel because I was drawing heavily on that one port engine and I wasn't sure that the cross-feed mechanism still worked to utilize the fuel in the starboard tank. But I switched the fuel-valve selectors to 'cross-feed' and held my breath. Fortunately it took and now all I had to worry about was flaps and gear upon landing.

"There was a 5,000 foot mountain range between me and Hollandia and I knew it didn't have enough gas to make it over that one, let alone climb to 5,000 feet. Fortunately, we had just captured a small island from the Japanese, called Wakde, 100 miles north and west of Hollandia and I decided to belly in there. I knew I couldn't put it down with gear and flaps or I would stall out. So I bellied in at the far end of the strip and stopped just a few hundred feet shy of going into the ocean.

"Hal Gray likes to kid me about this. There I was, sitting in the cockpit, finally stopped, smoke and dust everywhere and the first thing I did was to pull out my 'Form Five' (the official document that indicates the condition of the airplane). It was an automatic reaction, to write up the condition of the airplane so that the crew chief can go to work on it for the next day's mission. Suddenly, Hal, who had just landed, came running up. 'Get out, get out of

H. N. "Pete" Madison, with his P–38, Miss Fluff 'n Lace. Dennis Glen Cooper

there Pete, you're sitting in a bomb that could go up any minute,' and with that I dropped everything, unstrapped my parachute and got out. The plane was a write-off, but it did not catch fire.

"But it was an exceedingly easy airplane to fly as long as everything was going well. You know, it's a hands-off airplane once you get it trimmed up. So much so, that you would almost go to sleep coming back on those long missions where you are just boring holes through the sky and you are exhausted.

"So, we'd roll our windows down to let a little air in. There would be hours of sheer boredom fol-

John Mitchell, flight leader of the Yamamoto Mission on the left, and Rex Barber, pilot of the P–38 which apparently was the one whose guns shot down the Japanese admiral in his Betty bomber. The two former P–38 pilots gave a presentation at Santa Maria, California, on the fiftieth anniversary of the first P–38 flight.

lowed by the incredible excitement (and terror) of action."

The Yamamoto Mission—an interview with Rex Barber

Maj. John Mitchell, leader of the Yamamoto Mission, was quoted as saying, "There is no doubt in my mind that Rex Barber was the one who got Yamamoto."

Undoubtedly, the most stunning mission the P–38 ever flew in the South Pacific war was the one that resulted in the interception and shooting down of Adm. Isoroku Yamamoto, commander in chief of Japan's Combined Fleet in mid-April of 1943. The P–38 Lightning was the only aircraft in the Air Force inventory that had the range and the firepower to effectively deal with the challenge posed by this mission. Thus, Admiral Nimitz turned to the Air Force's 339th Fighter Squadron led by John Mitchell.

In January of 1989, on the fiftieth anniversary of the first flight of the P–38 prototype at Lockheed, a celebration was held at Santa Maria, California,

under the auspices of the Santa Maria Aviation Museum. P–38 veterans from all over the United States were there, including three of the surviving pilots from that famous mission. John Mitchell, now seventy-some years old, but fit and trim as if he were twenty years younger, gave an hour-long illustrated presentation of the Yamamoto Mission.

Present at the gathering were 339th pilots Rex Barber and James D. McClanahan. McClanahan had been forced to abort the mission because he blew a tire on takeoff, but Barber was one of the pilots that Mitchell had designated to be in the "killer" section of the flight. Over the years a controversy developed as to exactly which pilot in the killer section actually fired the bullets that shot down the admiral's plane. Credit for the kill had been awarded to Tom Lanphier, Jr., but Barber always felt deep in his heart that he was the one who actually did the deed.

Mitchell shared the podium with Barber. Behind them hung large maps of the Solomon Islands, and Mitchell opened the presentation by giving the audience some background: "The American Navy had broken the Japanese code and we had been listening to their top secret radio traffic since 1940." Mitchell explained that although this incredible feat did not help the United States avoid the Pearl Harbor debacle in 1941, it did pave the way for several successful encounters with the Japanese enemy, encounters like the Battle of Midway and the Yamamoto Mission—two battles which without a doubt affected the outcome of the war in the Pacific.

The P–38 was the airplane that Admiral Nimitz decided to use to destroy Yamamoto as soon as the US Navy learned that he would be making an inspection trip to the Solomon Islands. Specific details of his itinerary were gleaned from an intercepted radio message picked up in Hawaii on Apr. 13, 1943.

Within an hour the decoded message was on Nimitz's desk, the commander in chief of the US Pacific Fleet. Nimitz quickly decided that it was worth a try and passed the message on to Adm. William F. Halsey, who was the ranking American officer in the Solomon Islands area. Halsey convened a meeting of his staff and it was decided to award the mission to the Air Force, specifically to the 339th Fighter Squadron. At that time it was commanded by John Mitchell, and one of his best pilots was Rex Barber. I interviewed Barber in his Santa Maria hotel room after their presentation on the mission. Before going into detail on the mission, Barber described his first year with the Air Force after graduating from Flight School:

"I was sent to Hamilton Field, and got four hours on the P–40, that was the first fighter I had ever flown, and flew around the pattern, and a little bit of formation, and then on the fifth of December we were loaded onto the *President Monroe* that had just been commandeered for troop use. Two squad-

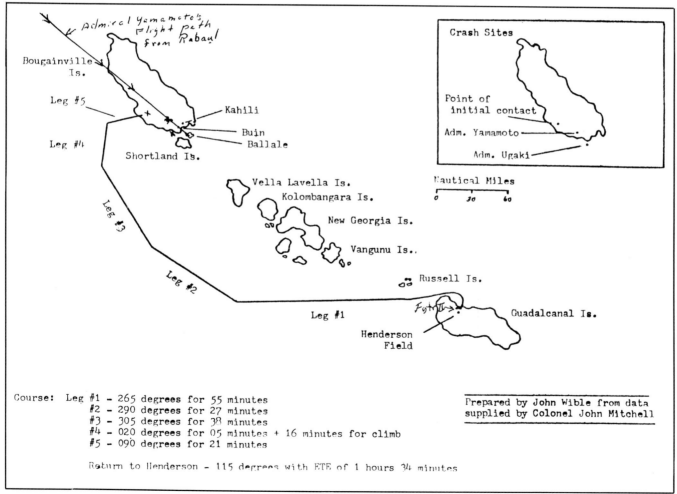

Course: Leg #1 – 265 degrees for 55 minutes
        #2 – 290 degrees for 27 minutes
        #3 – 305 degrees for 38 minutes
        #4 – 020 degrees for 05 minutes + 16 minutes for climb
        #5 – 090 degrees for 21 minutes

Return to Henderson – 115 degrees with ETE of 1 hours 34 minutes

Prepared by John Wible from data supplied by Colonel John Mitchell

Map of Yamamoto Mission drawn up by John Wible and supplied by Rex Barber.

rons of our group had already gone to the Philippines and the 70th Squadron and the 3rd Squadron, as well as the group headquarters, had been loaded onto this ship. We sailed out of San Francisco on the fifth of December, and got about halfway to Hawaii when the Japanese struck. We were given instructions to turn around and come back. We came back to port and unloaded and they reloaded us on another President line ship, the *President Garfield*, but this time, of course, it obviously wouldn't go to the Philippines so we joined a convoy. This convoy dropped off one ship at Christmas Island, one ship at Tonga and then our ship went on to Fiji, where we were to provide a perimeter defense to stop the Japanese from totally cutting our lines of communication to Australia and New Zealand.

"We got off the ship, and this time the aircraft we had in crates were P–39s. None of our enlisted men or anybody had ever seen or heard of a P–39 and we hadn't either, but fortunately there was a tech rep with us, who was a superman, and so we took the crates and got them uncrated up at a little airport; it was a grass strip actually. Of course, our men were very knowledgeable airmen, they had a lot of experience, and with the tech rep's guidance they took this new airplane and put it together rather quickly. We had those airplanes together in about two weeks. Vicellio was the Squadron Commander, and Mitchell was the Operations Officer. They had come from the 20th Fighter Group, which was also at Hamilton Field at that time.

"I then went from Fiji to Guadalcanal after it got started there, and we could get our airplanes in. They had built two fighter strips—Fighter Strip 1 for the Marines and Fighter Strip 2 for the Air Force, and then of course, Henderson Field which was built by the Japanese was there. So as quick as they could get airplanes in, they started running in detachments of pilots and crew people. We got our first P–38 in January, 1943.

Rex Barber, member of the killer section of the Yamamoto Mission, points to the area in which he and his fellow

P–38 pilots intercepted Admiral Yamamoto, the Japanese commander in chief, on Apr. 18, 1943.

Refueling on the strip in Hollandia, 475th Fighter Group.
Dennis Glen Cooper

"Compared to the 38s the 39 had relatively poor firepower for air-to-air combat, and it was not very maneuverable. It was not nearly as maneuverable as the 38 or the Zero, was not as fast as the Zero and we had to work together in order to avoid disaster. We managed, but then we got the 38s, and had the altitude advantage over the Zeroes, plus speed, and firepower.

"The P–38s came in with ferry pilots. They climbed on a transport and went home, and left the airplanes with us. We had the tech orders, which is an explanation of the airplane. We had a pilots manual which told us how to fly it, where the switches were, what they were, and what they were there for, etc. We got ourselves to where we figured we were quite well acquainted with the airplane, and got in and rolled it down the runway and took off. It was great. Good power, good maneuverability, easy to fly. Oh, it was a fine airplane, and it was so much better, so much more advanced than the P–39 that it was simply unbelievable.

"The only peculiarity the airplane had was when it was diving. If you dived it too fast your tail would start to flutter, and if you went too fast you got no response from your tail at all. If you had nerve enough to ride it down to lower altitude, you'd come out all right. You wanted to bring it out rather slowly because of the speed you were going. That was the only bad thing about the airplane, the inability to do a massive dive.

"One evening, in fact, it was the seventeenth of April, 1943, John Mitchell and Henry Vicellio (CO of the 70th Pursuit Group) and one other person came up to where we were bivouacked on the hill above the fighter strip on Guadalcanal. We were all sitting around there talking and it was about four or five o'clock, we were all through flying, and Vicellio

said 'Well, it's real important that you guys get a little rest tonight. I'd prefer you didn't drink any more of this "juice" that you have here. We've got a very important mission coming up tomorrow morning.' We accepted that and they drove off. They went over to Navy Headquarters on Henderson Field, Navy command up there under Admiral Mitscher. They were gone a couple of hours and then returned, and told us to be down in the operations tent in the morning at 5:00 for briefing. So at 5:00 the next morning, we went down, had breakfast and went over to the operations tent, where John Mitchell, who was to lead the mission, briefed us. He had selected the most qualified P–38 pilots. We had eighteen P–38s in commission. The Navy had flown in special 300 gallon bellytanks for us the night before. We had been using 165 gallon bellytanks so now we were able to increase our range tremendously by hanging a new 300 gallon tank on each airplane in addition to the normal tank. Our airmen had worked all night to get those special 300 gallon tanks hung and since we had never used them before they had to change a lot of the plumbing and did a marvelous job. I really don't know how they did it. We were told that the mission was to intercept Admiral Yamamoto's flight (we had cracked their secret radio code) which was coming down from Rabaul, New Guinea, to Ballale Island's landing strip.

"The mission, of course, was farther than any mission we'd ever run, that's why we had to have the extra tanks. Neither the Navy nor the Marines had planes with range enough to do the job, so that's why the P–38s were selected. Mitchell had some problems with figuring out just how to do it, but he knew that Yamamoto was coming down from Rabaul to Ballale and he knew the time of takeoff and the time of landing. So he then figured back the route from *Guadalcanal Fighter II* up to Empress Augusta Bay. Mitchell wanted to intercept him there. Mitchell of course had to figure out a lot of unknowns. He had to avoid a number of islands, all of which were Japanese-held. So that they wouldn't be alerted, we had to fly at fifty feet off the water. He figured the time it would take to go up there and where he wanted to intercept Yamamoto. He worked that out during the night. He had no real weather information, no wind information, except the Navy had told him that there was usually a five-knot wind coming from the west. He had to navigate up there by compass, his watch and his air speed, that's all. There were no radio aids to navigation in that area at that time. He flew so low (fifty feet off the deck) that he could not see any land. The only other time those

P–38s flew that low was when they were strafing something.

"Well, we got down to the operations tent and Mitchell had selected the pilots that he wanted on the mission. Kahili Airdrome was loaded with Zeroes, so we knew that there would be seventy-five or more Zeroes on that base, and we figured that they would be sending up an escort of honor to meet Yamamoto. Mitchell decided the best way to do it was to have two sections and a four-ship section called the killer section. He would take the rest of the airplanes upstairs and give us top cover from what we presumed would be a great many Zeroes. We knew there would be six of them with Yamamoto, but we weren't particularly concerned about six Zeroes. We *were* concerned about the fifty we expected to be up on top. He said 'All right, the killer section will go in on the bomber, and we'll take care of whatever's up above.' So he selected the pilots that he wanted to take, and he named Lanphier, myself, Joe Moore and [James] McClanahan as the killer section. He had eighteen airplanes in commission, so that meant that he was going to take twelve upstairs and our four would be sixteen, and

Close-up of ground crew working on 475th FG P–38. Notice that the starboard engine props are turning. Dennis Glen Cooper

he assigned Busby Holmes and Larry Hine to be the fill-in airplanes. They were to take anybody's position in the formation wherever it happened to be, if someone had to turn back. As we were taking off, McClanahan hooked a steel matting and blew a tire, and couldn't get off the ground. He was out.

"Mitchell had told us that just as quick as we got airborne, to turn on to our external tanks, and be sure they fed. We took off, and shortly after takeoff Joe Moore, the second man out of the killer section, couldn't get his new 300 gallon tank to feed. He tried two or three times and couldn't get any fuel out of it. So he had to turn back.

"Holmes and Hine then dropped in to killer section and became the second element. We just flew the legs as Mitchell had planned.

"Colonel Mitchell had borrowed a compass from the Navy the night before and had it 'swung' and mounted it in his cockpit as he wasn't totally confident in the P–38's compass. On takeoff, since he knew the heading of the runway, he was able to verify that the new compass was accurate.

"He laid the course out in five legs, all over water to avoid detection. The first leg was 265° for 55 minutes; second, 290° for 27 minutes; third, 305° for 38 minutes; fourth, 020° for 05 plus sixteen for climb; and fifth, 090° for 21 minutes.

"We were down to fifty feet off the water, and incredibly Mitchell hit landfall at his point up at Bougainville exactly one minute ahead of his schedule! This was an incredible feat. I don't know how anybody could navigate that closely and that precisely without any references. And just as we hit landfall, Doug Canning, who was leading the second element of Mitchell's flight, called: 'Bogies at eleven o'clock high,' and we looked up and sure enough there were the bombers, but there were *two* bombers instead of one, and up and behind them there were the six Zeroes, three on one side and three on the other. They were back quite a ways, obviously not expecting an attack. I think they were all kind of half asleep. So according to plan, Mitchell turned parallel to his course, and told Lanphier to take his killer section in for the attack. Well, Holmes tried to drop his tanks, but he couldn't get them to drop. So he and Ray Hine circled out over the water, while Tom and I bore on in on the Japanese. We were pretty close to a right angle.

"We got in fairly close to the bombers. The three Zeroes were on the right side and behind Yamamoto's bomber when we first sighted it, probably at 4,000 feet, and just as it had started to let down. We thought they had sighted us, but as it turns out from later information from the Japanese, they

had *not* sighted us. They were merely starting their letdown. Well, by the time we got to 2,500 feet or thereabouts, we were level with the bombers, and as we closed in, probably two or three miles from them, the three Zeroes on the right side broke down at us, very steeply, attempting to get between us and the bombers to shoot us down. We could see that they would be right on our tail just about the time we turned in on the bombers, and probably shoot us down immediately. So at the last minute Tom broke at right angles and flew up into the Zeroes. I went right on in and immediately banked up to get on the bomber's tail. I was quite close, a little too close, as they were going downhill. They were probably down to 1,500 or 1,200 feet or maybe even 1,000 feet by that time, and I had gained a bit of speed, so when I banked up, I banked up sharply and pulled around very tight, and lost sight of the 'two' bombers under my wing. When I rolled back there was a bomber, a 'Betty,' sitting just to the right of me. I didn't know where the other one was. So I commenced shooting at this one bomber. I was to the left and I shot over the fuselage into his right engine, and then pulled in right behind him, very close to him, and shot into his right engine some more, and then back into the fuselage, then into the left engine. There was no fire from the bomber, whatsoever.

"About this time he snapped up, slowing rapidly, and I presume he lost one engine; the right engine by that time was smoking very black smoke. I shot over him and looked back to see what happened and I could see him banked up and that three Zeroes were right on *my* tail. The other flight of three Zeroes had broken down and had caught me by that time, so I ducked and went out toward the coast, and got right down on the treetops, and I would skid back and forth as they started to shoot, making passes at me.

"The P–38 in straight and level flight is a little bit faster than the Zero, so I started to pull away from them, and I was heading south to get out of the area. But as I was starting to approach the coast, I saw a bomber right on the water. He was so close to the water that his props were kicking up wakes, they weren't touching the water; they were blowing a wake out, and about that time I saw Holmes and Hine circling out over the ocean and they sighted the bomber too. So they dived down on him and got there before I did. Ray Hine was flying very close formation as Holmes started to shoot. His bullets hit the water back of the bomber. Hines started to shoot also, and his bullets hit outside the wing, but he was at so close a formation that he couldn't really make a

The location of this particular scene is not clear; however, most probably it is in the Solomon Islands. The wrecked Japanese aircraft have been bombed and strafed by P-38s from the 475th Fighter Group. Dennis Glen Cooper

gunnery pass. So Holmes walked the fire right up through the right engine, and on out beyond the airplane. As he passed through the right engine, white vapor started to come off the trailing edge of the wing, which I presume meant he had punctured a tank, but hadn't set it on fire. So I came in and dropped in directly behind the bomber, and got very close to him and opened fire. Almost immediately he exploded, and crashed into the ocean. A big piece of [the Japanese bomber] flew up and cut through my right intercooler and another large chunk hit my canopy and cut a big slash in it.

"To go back to where we made the initial attack, I didn't know where the second bomber went. Lanphier claimed that a bomber circled underneath him, and he was up on his back at 6,000 feet and came down and shot it down. Well, I couldn't deny it. I didn't know what happened to the other bomber, so when we got back, Lanphier claimed a bomber, I claimed a bomber and Holmes claimed a bomber, or Holmes and I claimed a bomber over the water.

"Now as we get information from the Japanese, we find out that there were only two bombers. Somebody was wrong. The reason I never could contradict Lanphier was because I did not know where that second bomber had turned to, and it wasn't until I read *The Reluctant Admiral* that a lot of problems were solved, because I knew some of the things that were being said weren't accurate, but I had no way of proving it. But what happened was

that when I backed up and lost track of the airplanes, I rolled over and was sitting right on top of the second bomber. He was still in formation. The first that they knew about the attack was when they saw tracers going over their canopy into Yamamoto's airplane; the crew chief pointed up and said 'enemy aircraft.' He looked up and saw the P-38 sitting right on top of him, so he went down and out to sea. That solved the problem of where the second bomber went. It was obvious that no bomber had circled under Lanphier. Three people lived through the crash of the second Betty—three Japanese.

"You see, originally, we thought there were three airplanes; Lanphier said one turned and went underneath him, and he went up through the Zeroes, rolled over on his back at 6,000 feet and looked down and saw this bomber over the jungle and he peeled off and went down and shot a wing off of him. He claimed it was the lead bomber. Well, I didn't know, and I'm a little reluctant to go around claiming things I don't know . . .

"Well, the thing is, you see, the bomber that crashed inland, they got Yamamoto's body out of it the next day, so obviously that was the bomber that went in. And then the Japanese pilot who was in one of the Zeroes behind us explained exactly how the airplane was shot down . . . It was attacked immediately; it went straight ahead, streaming black smoke, then fire, then it crashed into the jungle. And so that answered that question.

"Yamamoto's Chief of Staff, [Hiroyuki] Agawa, was riding in the second bomber. He lived through the crash. The pilot lived through the crash, and one of the airmen lived through it. The others were all killed, and so, we know that there were two bombers that came down, no third bomber. All this came to light with Yanagiya's tape, he was the Japanese Zero pilot the Sony Corporation interviewed in Japan back in 1975. We didn't know anything about this until we were down at the Admiral Nimitz Museum in Fredericksburg, Texas, where Yanagiya's tape had been dubbed in with Mitchell's and my tape, and made it very obvious as to what had happened."

Another veteran of the 475th Fighter Group, P. J. Dahl, who flew 283 missions in the P-38 in the Pacific, had this to say about the airplane: "The only drawback was its poor rearward vision. We often said that the cockpit was facing the wrong way. But its great advantage was its twin-engine capability. If I were being attacked I could if I wanted to simply turn the airplane on its wing tip and put the engine and all that metal between me and the other guy. It gave you a great feeling of security."

54

"What an airplane! I'm glad we met."

Dear Jesse,

Here are some notes that may explain how my love affair with the P–38 got started:

Oddly enough, it begins with the P–47 Thunderbolt. I was squadron commander of the 340th Fighter Squadron of the 348th Fighter Group, the first of the P–47s to be sent to the southwest Pacific area. We off loaded at Brisbane, Australia, and began assembly and flight testing the aircraft at an Australian airfield called Charters Towers.

Not far away, at Amberly Airfield, the 475th Fighter Group was doing essentially the same thing. General George Kenney, commander of the Far East Air Force, under General MacArthur, had been cleared to form an all P–38 group providing he could do it from his own resources. The key personnel had come from other fighter groups in the Fifth Air Force, and the aircraft came from the P–38 replacement pool. The result was a unique fighter group, wholly formed in the theater and destined to become the backbone of fighter operations in the Fifth Air Force. The man largely responsible for the smooth beginning of this group was Colonel George Prentice, a veteran combat pilot, respected and admired by all who knew him.

By July 1943, I had taken my P–47 Squadron north to Port Moresby, New Guinea, where we had begun operations out of Seven Mile Airstrip.

Things happen fast in a war. And not always the way you anticipate. I was promoted to Lieutenant Colonel and assigned to the 475th Group which in September was flying out of Dobadura, across the Owen Stanley Range from Port Moresby. I checked in as deputy commander to George Prentice and lost no time in getting checked out in the P–38.

Since I was considered an experienced pilot there wasn't much to it. No ground school; there weren't any two seater P–38s. I just sat in the cockpit and got familiar with where all the essentials were located. Then the squadron Operations Officer got up on the wing, stuck his head in and answered questions, and pointed out a few idiosyncrasies, such as you have to push this little button before you can move the landing gear control. Then he showed me how to start the engines, after which, he climbed down. The crew chief pulled the wheel chocks and I taxied out to the runway.

There was a satisfying surge of power as I advanced the throttles, and after a remarkably short run I was airborne. I headed out to sea, climbing to around 12,000 feet. I did a series of stall maneuvers under all possible configurations with power on and power off. At this point I really began to like this airplane. It was completely honest; no sneaky tricks like trying to swerve into a spin or a flip, and most of the time there was ample warning. It was like the plane saying: "Hey, you dummy, you're about to go into a full stall." And I replied, "I know, I want to see what you'll do."

Then I tried some high speed runs and climbs leading into a series of aerobatics. By now I was sweating profusely and the airplane wasn't even breathing hard. I trimmed her up for straight and level (the P–38, properly trimmed, would fly herself with very little attention), leaned back in the seat and lit a cigarette. I thought, "Baby, you and I are going to get along just fine." Later, I stubbed the cigarette out on my heel and put the butt in my pocket, thinking when I get a P–38 assigned to me I'll have the crew chief put an ashtray in here. One with a lid on it so the butts and ashes won't fall out when I'm upside down.

After I had landed and parked, the operations officer came out and asked, "How'd it go?" I said, "Couldn't be better."

That began a long association, from 1943 to 1945, with more than 200 combat missions. We survived many bullet holes; a mid-air bath in Japanese crankcase oil; on occasion, pieces of Japanese aircraft aluminum in the air intakes; and of course some awfully foul weather.

What an airplane! I'm glad we met.

Sincerely,

Charles MacDonald

Chapter 4

The Restoration of *Joltin' Josie*

Lockheed twenty-nine Quebec is the call sign. *Joltin' Josie* is the P-38's name. It came off the Lockheed Burbank assembly line as a P-38J in mid 1944, was flight tested and then delivered to the Air Force in June. *Josie* remained in the Air Force inventory without going overseas. Details of the airplane's assignment are unclear, but undoubtedly it served as a training aircraft and then after the war was purchased by a flight school in Santa Maria, California. *Josie* served there as a training aid like so many surplus aircraft from World War II.

A few years later a collector bought the plane, painted it black and that was the way Ed Maloney found it, parked in the weeds at Brackett Field at La Verne, California. "There were thousands of airplanes in the government's inventory at the end of the war," Maloney said. "Many of them went up for sale, and if you were lucky, and at the right spot at the right time, you could get one at a very reasonable price." He was obviously at the right spot at the right time. For less than $2,000 Maloney found himself the owner of a P-38 Lightning. That was almost twenty-five years ago.

Today there are probably no more than two dozen Lightnings in existence. Most are in museums or "on a pole somewhere" as one researcher remarked. And now that the Chino plane is flying, that makes seven or possibly eight in the world that are actually flyable. A total of 9,982 Lightnings had been made by the end of World War II and thousands wound up on the scrap heap—all of which makes a flyable P-38 a national treasure. We are fortunate to have farsighted people like Ed Maloney and Bob Pond involved in preserving these great examples of our aviation heritage.

Maloney was able to remove the new acquisition to his Planes of Fame Museum then in Ontario, California, where he put it on static display. A few years later the museum moved to Chino and the P-38 had to be towed to its new destination. Unfortunately, a tow bar broke in transit, resulting in a collapsed nose gear, damaging the nose.

The plane sat outside the museum for almost twenty years gathering dust, subject to the constant wear and tear of the elements. Finally, Maloney saw his way clear to start the restoration. Several major sponsors were enlisted, funds were raised and the time came in mid 1987 to bring *Joltin' Josie* back to life.

After the annual Planes of Fame Air Show that year, the P-38 was slowly and carefully towed into the yard in front of Fighter Rebuilders among the other warbirds. By that time, Steve Hinton had hired a new man to his force, John Kagihara, or JK, who, with Rich Palmer, was assigned full-time to the Lightning rebuild.

Disassembly

"The secret is to have just one or two men on the job during the disassembly process. One person is responsible for all the parts that come off the airplane. Everything gets put into one area, and you make *lots* of lists," said Steve Hinton. Rich Palmer made it sound a bit more challenging: "We had a large number of those big trash barrels which you've seen around the shop. They were set aside specifically for P-38 parts. Different pieces went into different barrels and it seemed to work for a while. Then one night, one of the guys was cleaning up, dumping trash, and guess what, a whole barrel of P-38 parts got dumped. Well, we really freaked out over that one. But fortunately it was just an isolated incident."

Another point that Hinton made about the disassembly process was that the person in charge of the project must have an excellent memory. Also, as certain components come off the plane they are not taken apart until needed. Subsystems are kept intact until it becomes time to actually repair them or to send them out for rebuild. When the P-38's radiators went out for pressure testing and overhaul, the important sealing strips that go along with them were lost at the cad-plating shop and had to be specially fabricated much later by Rich Palmer.

I asked Ed Maloney his thoughts about the restoration: "Well, you can't do this thing in a halfway fashion, particularly with a warbird and certainly not with a P-38. We decided to go through it completely, replace all the systems, clean up all the corrosion and make it as near new as possible. There are miles and miles of coolant tubing in there and since it's under pressure we felt it necessary to replace it all because after so many years you put pressure on those lines and it's literally just like a showerhead. The plane is not an easy one to work on. It's great to fly, but ask any mechanic and they will say it's a bear to work on. We decided not to take any chances and do a complete rebuild."

"We call it an IRAN," said Hinton, "inspected and repaired as necessary. This P–38 was all there. It just needed to be completely disassembled and rebuilt. Fuel lines, hydraulic lines, fuel tanks, electrical wiring, everything was replaced."

With all the electrical wires pulled and discarded, all the fuel, vacuum, coolant, oil and hydraulic lines off, the plane had been essentially gutted. The original fuel tanks were taken out and discarded and an order for new ones was issued.

The canopy was removed and disassembled. All the cockpit instruments came out and everything was laid bare so that the entire airplane could be carefully scrutinized for corrosion.

"And corrosion we found," said Rich Palmer. "There was a very bad spot back at the tail where the rudders join the boom, particularly on the right side, and we were forced to totally redo that area."

The two original Allison engines were not taken completely off until the aircraft had been pushed inside the shop's hangar. They were left hanging on their mounts (for weight and balance purposes) until the P–38 was put onto jacks.

Joltin' Josie *as she was "before," on static display at Planes of Fame Museum prior to restoration.* Frank Mormillo

Joltin' Josie *prior to the restoration. The gun doors are off and the gun-mount structure is visible. These components* were not included in the rebuild in the interest of weight reduction. Frank Mormillo

57

The left-hand wing panel just removed from the aircraft. The cowling will attach where the bent sheet metal is seen *on the front edge. At the bottom of the wing in front is the attachment point for the engine mount.*

Up on jacks

"While most tricycle gear aircraft have a jack point on the nose and jack points on the wings, the P–38 is unique in that the book tells you to make a

The P–38J in the Fighter Rebuilders shop before the engines and landing gear have been removed for rebuild. Planes of Fame

heavy weight, a tripod stanchion, and put a bolt in the tail, tying it to the tripod weight unit," according to Rich Palmer. "This keeps the tail down when the wing is jacked up and eliminates the need for a nose jack, thus freeing up that work space. That is the Lockheed way of doing things.

"One really goes by the book on a lot of things; there are many manuals and references, but accurate restorations from the point of view of how the aircraft rolled off the assembly line are not what Fighter Rebuilders at Chino is all about. Rather, there is much modernization that goes on in the process. Systems, components and avionics are ways to make the aircraft as reliable as possible, relative to today's setting. Typically, engines will be of a later model than the original plane because a later engine type simply works better. Later model components or systems work the best, and are more reliable. The earlier engines are less reliable, with less power. With later model engines, systems and components, there is the benefit of technology evolved for that particular engine. Used in the earlier P–38 were the 50 or 60 series Allison. The 111s

Inside the shop at Chino, you can see the part of the support system for holding down the airplane. The jack on top of the drum is screwed into a fitting on the rear of the *boom. The barrel is filled with water and the supports are welded onto the heavy barrel. Note the trash barrel to the right filled with metal trim pieces.*

and the 113s are what are being used here. These were the last Allisons that were built," continued Palmer.

The disassembly process at Chino went on at a steady pace. Some components came off with a minimum of effort and some did not. The wing removal turned out to be a struggle because corrosion and rust had caused many of the bushings and attachment points to be locked up solid. With the airplane finally up on jacks, the two airframe mechanics found themselves frequently having to stop work and take time to carefully analyze a particular problem.

"That's the way it was with the wings," observed John Kagihara. "We finally got them off but it was a tough process. We used lots of WD-40 and it took lots of pushing and shoving. But they finally came off and we put them in storage until we were ready for them at the end of the rebuild."

The plane was slowly, carefully and totally disassembled down to the fuselage center section which was left intact. The tail section was removed

and taken apart. All the hardware came off and pieces that required cadmium plating were sent out to the plating shop. The radiators were rebuilt and pressure tested.

With the P–38 now in pieces, the engines gone and the landing gear off, the cleaning and brightening process began in earnest. As John Kagihara said, "It was a process of take it off, check it out and clean it up." Old rivets were removed with a power drill. A bit exactly the same size as the original hole was used. "We didn't want to damage the metal or enlarge the hole any more than it already was," said Kagihara.

The disassembly process was also an inspection process. The air frame was stripped to a point where any damage and corrosion could be spotted and repaired.

Engine rebuild

The engines were recrated and sent to John Sandberg's shop in Minneapolis, Minnesota, for rebuilding. Sandberg exchanged the original engines from *Joltin' Josie* for a pair of new Allisons that he had on hand. Sandberg, the owner of JRS Enterprises, is perhaps better known for his unlimited air racer, *Tsunami*. However, if you have a warbird and need an engine rebuild, he is your man.

JRS Enterprises is located in a 3,500 square foot space in the rear of a building that houses a separate company, Metal Masters (a manufacturer and designer of disk drive spindles for the computer industry). The engine rebuild company has been in business since 1970 and Sandberg prides himself on being the only company in the world that is totally dedicated to the warbird industry.

When I visited JRS Enterprises, there were a number of aircraft engines sitting out in the grass behind the shop either being used as a source for parts or waiting their turn to be brought back to life. Inside, Bill Moja was working on a Wright 3350 while Sam Torvik was busy at detail work on engine components.

I interviewed Sandberg in his office and he spoke with pride about his operation: "There is no one that specializes in the warbird industry except us. We do everything from 985s (a 450 bph Pratt and Whitney for the Staggerwing or Twin Beech) up to Allisons and Merlins and round engines as well. We try to tailor the rebuild around the people who are going to be using the airplane. What we have done is develop special ring and piston combinations and bearing clearances and methods of assembly that we don't have problems with.

"A typical Allison rebuild takes about 340 hours. We completely disassemble the engine and go through it from top to bottom," said Sandberg. "We inspect it thoroughly via magnetic particle inspection and then we reassemble the engine, using reprocessed bearings, replacing the existing shells, as well as the bushings and the rods. The liners are honed to size, the valves are taken out and completely done over. The reduction gear and accessory drives are all rebuilt and the supercharger is completely rebuilt. All accessories such as the magnetos and distributors are rebuilt along with the ignition harness. And the water pump is rebuilt.

An early rebuild shot looking forward. As you can see, no radiators have been installed. Exhaust components are on the floor at the left.

"We've gone into a lot of parts manufacture to make these rebuilds work. We've commissioned molds for rubber parts and gaskets, crank and prop shaft seals—all that is stuff we've had made. The way the military ran these engines was different from the kind of use they get today. The Air Corps ran them for lots of hours in a short time. A warbird today may run seventy to eighty hours per year so what we do is set the tolerances up and make sure we get lots of oil flow through the bearings to preclude any failures, say on a 'dry start' or something like that if the airplane has been sitting for a long time. Then, after the rebuild we put it on the test stand for six hours and run it right through the full range of power settings right up to 'war emergency.'

"Remember, a World War II Allison would have a normal oil consumption of anything from two to five gallons an hour. This was perfectly acceptable then, but not for the purists that we are dealing with today. Typically, an Allison that we rebuild will use less than a quart of oil an hour. Merlins even less."

Sandberg has five employees. Two of them—shop foreman, Bill Moja, the "round" engine specialist and Sam Torvik, the Merlin specialist—have worked for Sandberg since the business started. "We more or less learned it together," said Sandberg.

What JRS Enterprises' neighbors complain about the most is the noise from the outdoor engine test stand. "We run the engines on the test stand for six hours. We run for a long time at what we consider normal cruise power and then we run them through complete idle and then takeoff and through various configurations to simulate the exact operation of the airplane. For takeoff we will use a two-minute configuration, a climb power for ten minutes, then cruise power for an hour. We try to simulate all this ahead of time so that if any problems show up they will show up on the test stand and not on the airplane," said Sandberg.

John Sandberg, president of JRS Enterprises in Minneapolis, poses for the camera next to a big round engine, as the Wright 3350 radials are known to warbird enthusiasts. Sandberg owns one of the few companies in the world whose business is dedicated to the rebuilding of warbird powerplants. The engines for Joltin' Josie came out of Sandberg's shop, as do many of the engines that are installed in the planes restored by Fighter Rebuilders.

Bill Moja, the chief mechanic at JRS Enterprises in Minneapolis, Minnesota, is holding a crankshaft for the Allison V–12.

When I spoke to him recently on the phone, he was just leaving for a meeting with neighbors who were complaining about his activity. Sandberg commented: "We've been grandfathered in here, but we have to move and we plan to expand the shop to a 16,000 square foot facility at Buffalo, Minnesota. We'll be able to hire more people to help us deal with all the work."

The rebuilt Allisons develop 1425 bhp at sixty inches of mercury and 3000 rpm. This is without the turbochargers. In the turbo configuration the Allisons were rated at 1600 bhp with water injection. The reasons for not using the turbochargers were primarily practical ones. As Sandberg pointed out, "The turbo wheels themselves have a tendency to throw a blade once in a while." Another reason for not using the turbos was the simple fact that the P–38 was not going to be flown at 30,000 feet as it was in wartime. The turbos would be helpful at 30,000 feet but less so at lower elevations, and from the maintenance standpoint it made much more sense to do without. (Sandberg pointed out that on the

Sam Torvik, in the process of deburring a Rolls-Royce Merlin piston, is putting a radius on the ring grooves.

B–17 you almost *have* to use the turbochargers because you can't get takeoff horsepower without them. They use the same turbo that is used on the P–38 and the B–24.) Also, there is a major weight savings, in the neighborhood of 150 pounds per engine.

Sheet metal

The principal culprit in sheet metal problems with warbird restoration is bi-metal corrosion and so-called hangar damage. On *Joltin' Josie* it was mostly dissimilar metal corrosion that needed attention.

"There was a very bad spot back at the tail where the rudders join the boom, particularly on the right side and we were forced to totally redo that area. *Josie* was not nearly as bad as Stephen Grey's P–38 (due to fly in the summer of 1990) which had a lot of damage to the tail and wing surfaces from people taking axes and other blunt instruments to the metal, apparently in an effort to salvage parts. But with *Josie*, aside from the significant corrosion in the tail and the total rebuild of the nose due to

damage from a towing accident many years ago, we didn't have that much of a problem," said Rich Palmer.

Joltin' Josie was built in the spring of 1944 and at that point Lockheed was not zincing any of the sheet metal, nor was there any other treatment carried out to protect the airplane from corrosion due to the simple fact that they thought the average life of the airplane was going to be so short that such effort was not necessary. The absence of a zinc chromate primer or an "al clad" layer (pure aluminum over the alloy) created a very vulnerable surface to the effects of corrosion. But *Josie* was not in bad shape and with "brightener" and the simple replacement of sheet metal in the few areas that required it, she came out well. (Rich Palmer commented at his astonishment when on Stephen Grey's P–38 he buffed off the paint and zinc to find he was able to see his reflection in the fifty-year-old aluminum sheet metal.)

"We had a lot of what we call 'crusties'—small areas of surface corrosion that flake off with a finger or a knife. With an aluminum etching agent and

Sandberg's back yard at JRS Enterprises, with a rough Allison sitting ready to be overhauled. Two Wright 3350 radial engines are in the background. These were used on a wide variety of aircraft—B–29s, DC–7s and Douglas Skyraiders.

brightener you can clean the corrosion right off the skin," said Palmer. "So basically what we do is look for corrosion, clean it up, brighten it and then paint it. And on *Josie,* since many of the parts were not zinced and with two different kinds of metal sitting on top of each other, moisture gets in between them and that is when you have a problem. Sometimes the corrosion will actually grow and puff up, even to the extent of popping rivets. So that is one of the ways we look for that kind of damage, looking for areas that have popped rivets or slightly puffed up surfaces.

"We would use templates for areas that had been badly damaged, dropped or vandalized and this was the case with the nose of the airplane. We had some areas on the wings that needed work, but it was not that significant. It's called R&R—remove and replace."

Palmer continued: "We use a so-called English roller which is a fairly common tool in working with sheet metal and it's basically a tool with two steel wheels: a flat wheel plus a second wheel that has a round surface and when you put those two together the point of contact applies pressure to the metal. It pushes on the metal and [shapes] the aluminum the

way we want it to go. The aluminum on the engine cowling, for example, is softer aluminum than on the wing and very vulnerable to [damage] where people had been climbing on the [cowling]. And all we do is put the piece into the English roller and hammer it out and bring it back to the way it should be."

For Rich Palmer, the whole project proved to be more challenging than he had expected. He had worked briefly on the other P–38 at Fighter Rebuilders, the one owned by Stephen Grey—a well-known English collector—but this was his first total rebuild on a Lightning. "It was worse than we expected, in terms of corrosion," Palmer said later. "We found significant corrosion in the tail structure and that involved more work than had been planned.

"What we hadn't expected, however, was the need to replace all the control cables. They were all bad and had to go. With the P–38, that's a big deal. With the combination of the tight quarters, plus the fact that there are two tail booms, and two sets of rudder cables going to each side of the elevator, you've got two of everything, all adjusted by means of turnbarrels located at strategic points where they can be disconnected. There are as many as five

Bill Moja uses a fork lift to move an Allison into the shop. The engine shown here is one that was taken off of Joltin' Josie *prior to the rebuild. JRS then supplied Fighter*

Rebuilders with two other identical Allisons that had been rebuilt at their shop and were ready to go.

The scene at JRS, when an Allison engine is put through its paces on the test stand. The engines are run through their full range of power up to war emergency, and are on the stand for six hours before being signed off. This back *yard scene belies the efficiency and great attention to detail that goes into the rebuild of one of these engines.* Janet Bjornstad

Joltin' Josie *at an early stage of her rebuild. The pilot's seat sits on the wing to the left of the cockpit. The pilot's folding ladder is at the rear of the cockpit pod. The large*

empty space at the rear of the cockpit on the main spar is where the hydraulic pump is located. The hydraulic fluid tank access hole is ahead of it, near the back of the canopy.

turn-barrels on each cable to be adjusted. There has to be just the right amount of tension, measured by a cable tension meter, adjusted not only for position but for tension.

"Compared to a Mustang, for example, the Lightning is much more complicated. There is more distance to travel and the basic design is more complex. The cramped quarters of working inside the spar or the boom or the wheelwells only adds to the challenge. The complex web includes cables going down the spar, to each side of the airplane and to the tail. We were constantly referring to the Lockheed manual, trying to figure out which pulley goes to which cable. It was a combination of going by the book and by the seat of the pants. But we could not have done the job without the Lockheed books," commented Palmer.

Scavenging parts

On one of my first visits to the shop I noticed a flatbed truck parked outside, burdened down with a load of bent and twisted, dirty, rusting scrap metal. It

turned out that Steve Hinton's crew had just come back from the site of a P–38 wreck near Los Alamos, California, where a plane that was being used in photo survey work had crashed many years ago. Finding the wreck was a major project, but arrangements were made to salvage what they could. Escalating restoration costs and the scarcity of parts make such wrecks interesting to the restorer. As I looked over the tangled mess of filthy, corroded steel and aluminum, it was inconceivable to me that any of it would be usable.

The only salvaged parts from the wrecked Lightning that found their way into *Joltin' Josie* were a few small pieces used on the rebuilt canopy latch mechanism.

Engine installation

By March of 1988 both engines were back from JRS Enterprises and ready to be installed.

When it came time to install the port engine, a lot of other jobs had to be completed. Prior to the installation, all the pieces of airplane that fit directly

66

behind the engine such as the oil tank and various control lines to the wing area had to be installed and completed. It's a snug fit and when the fork lift guided by Hinton slowly positioned the engine into place, there was a lot of grunting and shoving by the assembled team.

Rich Palmer recalled: "It's a tight installation, particularly between the back of the engine and the oil tank. Before we could install the engine, the majority of the hydraulic lines had to be finished because part of the engine mount also holds the landing gear actuator. Oil tanks were all done and painted. Once the engine is on, it's almost like a domino effect because then the big ducts for the front air intakes can be fitted and all kinds of things can begin to get done. Oil lines, water lines, hydraulic lines, vacuum pumps all can then be hooked up. Then come the cowl formers, then the cowling itself and then all the work can start on shaping the cowlings and making sure everything fits the way it should. So the engine installation is a major milestone towards completion of the rebuild."

Turbos and exhausts

It was never Steve Hinton's intention to have operating turbochargers on *Joltin' Josie*. There were several reasons for this, but primarily it was decided on the basis of ease of maintenance. As John Sand-

Stephen Grey's airplane. This is the area around the turbocharger and shows well the electrolysis and corrosion that occurs between two dissimilar metals. Essentially, the aluminum has dissolved away. Joltin' Josie *sustained similar damage which Fighter Rebuilders repaired.*

This tail came off of Grey's Lightning, and its damaged condition is typical of what Fighter Rebuilders has to work with these days. The two gouges (left center) are undoubt- *edly the result of a hatchet or other blunt tool. But components such as these can be made to look like new by the skilled sheet metal people at Fighter Rebuilders.*

A view of the top of the wing showing the type of damage that is typical these days, when someone needing flap components used a hatchet to cut a hole and remove needed parts. Holes are shot in the wing. The corrosion is espe- *cially bad forward. The piece on the left fell apart in Rich Palmer's hand upon removal. There is also visual evidence of severe corrosion next to the stainless steel in the foreground.*

berg of JRS pointed out, the P–38's turbochargers were not only *old*, but old technology and "have a tendency to throw a blade once in a while." Further, the airplane was not going to be flown very often at the high altitudes where turbos are necessary.

Rich Palmer had this to say: "As you [may] know, the Allisons have an internal supercharger and there are different gear ratios that you can fit to that supercharger. So we put a higher blower gear ratio in each of them to compensate for the absence of the turbo. In addition, by not having to overhaul the turbo system we saved months of work, not to mention the cost of it all, plus the headaches down the road maintaining the system. And it's a great

weight-saver. We ran all stock exhausts and where the turbos are fitted up on top we simply removed the compressor wheel and the exhaust section and were left with a gutted turbo. The top part of the turbo section had the actual bolts for mounting it into the airplane so we left the bottom part off and bolted the rest back into the airplane. It looks stock but all it does is flow exhaust through there.

"We also left off the intercoolers, which were on the stock airplane up forward underneath the engine. We just simply covered the area with a plate and ran the air right up into the carburetors. Without the turbos there was no reason to have an intercooler. Yet, the airplane looks stock as we left the 'footballs' (the turbo intakes on the side of the aircraft) on there and to the casual observer it looks like we've got operating turbos.

"But we still had a problem to figure out how to [duct] the air to the carburetors. One day I was driving down the freeway and there was a big semi-truck right next to me and I looked over at him and noticed these large rubber hoses that were obviously carrying the air into his carburetors, so I went right down to the truck store and came back to the shop with an armful of big, six-inch-diameter rubber elbows, ninety degrees and forty-five degrees. We still had to make some round tubing out of aluminum to use between the rubber elbows, but it worked just fine."

Hydraulic system

One of my most vivid memories from documenting the rebuild of *Joltin' Josie* was the sight of Kevin Eldridge working away day after day building up the many hundreds of feet of hydraulic lines for the airplane. In addition to the set for *Josie*, he made an additional set for the second P–38, waiting for its rebuild. It was tedious work, but Eldridge was the man assigned to fabricate and install all of the hydraulic lines.

Precision and care were the watch words as all the countless fittings came together, and eventually the network of tubing was complete and ready to be tested. Hydraulic leaks are rare due to the well-designed connectors, and the system worked perfectly as soon as it was switched on. Capacity of the hydraulic system is 8 gallons. Fluid used is a 56–06 military specification type.

Electrical system

All the original electrical wiring in the P–38 was ripped out and thrown away. It was totally replaced

Needed parts are being identified from a crashed P–38 recovered from a site near Los Alamos, California. The Lightning went down in a cow pasture sometime in the mid 1960s. It had been an aerial photo and mapping plane. The landing gear is sitting on the rear of the flatbed trailer. The ball bearings on the axle can be seen, as well as the retract mechanism which Rich Palmer is examining. Jim Dale and Matt Nightingale are working on a spar section of the wing. Lockheed built a very tough airplane and there were quite a few parts to be salvaged from this aircraft.

The main landing gear doors are in the lower right of the picture just above the gear doors in the bottom of the flap area. It is hard to say whether this is an inboard or outboard wing.

with new wire, personally fitted and installed by Steve Hinton.

As Rich Palmer explained: "Steve has a way with electrical systems and it was his baby. You don't bother him when he's working on the electrics. On the stock P–38 they used cannon plugs extensively. Well, we attempted to get rid of all the cannon plugs and if the wire goes from the cockpit all the way back to the tail, it's going to be all one wire. That's a new way to go about it. And we also modified the coolant door actuators over from hydraulic to electrically operated units out of a Mustang. In the old days there was a huge great wiring bundle for the radio system. Well, we tossed all that and made it a much simpler setup, with the navcom set up in the cockpit.

"The radio hookup was done by the radio specialist at Chino airport, and all the circuit breakers were located in the cockpit. A set of dashboard lights were installed that show the position of the landing gear. Micro switches for the landing gear positions are all installed as well. Wire was run for all the usual lights needed, but the absence of an anticollision light precluded the plane's use at night."

Cooling system

During disassembly all the original coolant lines were pulled out of the airplane and discarded. New ones were manufactured using the old ones as templates. These new aluminum lines were then patiently reinstalled.

There are several different size coolant lines on the Lightning. Lines of 1¾ and 2½ inches go through the wheelwells. These were painted blue and presented a striking visual presentation as you looked up into the wheelwell. The coolant (100 percent Prestone) flows out of the engines and to the radiators through one 1¾ inch line on each side. There they are combined and the flow is taken back to the engine through the large 2½ inch line in the wheelwell.

On the P–38 each engine has two coolant radiators and one water pump located under each engine. In the rebuild operation, *Josie's* four radiators were inspected visually and then removed. Out of an existing inventory of P–38 radiators, Fighter Rebuilders found four that were serviceable and not in need of recoring. (Recoring would have been expensive; one shop wanted upwards of several thousand dollars for the job.) Before fitting the two radiators that were chosen for the installation they were pressure tested according to Lockheed specifications.

The coolant doors came off the airplane, were cleaned up and then refitted, but with electrically operated actuators.

These doors open and close to regulate the flow of air. When more power is pulled, more heat is generated and therefore more cooling is necessary. For instance, on takeoffs when the ambient air temperature is high, the radiator doors are open. The pilot is able to control them either manually or allow them to work automatically.

The stock P–38J had a hydraulically operated coolant door system but this was a disadvantage. If the hydraulics failed, the plane was left with doors either fully open or fully closed. In normal operation the doors are in between these two extremes. With no in-between setting the engine runs either too hot or too cold. The new system works effi-

ciently, however, with the airplane running "real cool" according to Rich Palmer. It is pressurized at 17 psi.

The radiators on the P–38 grew as it developed. On the prototype, they were located inside the booms with an intake scoop on the bottom and an exit door at the rear, like on a P–51 Mustang. As more and more power was extracted from the Allisons, larger capacity radiators were needed.

Fuel system

Josie's original fuel tanks were of a heavy, self-sealing design. A gel-like substance was sandwiched between the outer and inner layer of rubber that formed the tank. The gel expanded if it contacted fuel. When a bullet penetrated the tank and gasoline leaked into the gel, the gel expanded to close the hole. The hole could be repaired easily back at the base by putting a piece of rubber in the hole.

These original fuel cells had rotted and were suitable only for use as templates for new bladder tanks that were manufactured by Henry Krug of

Kevin Eldridge is just a blur, he is working so fast. Rich Palmer is working on the main fuel tank area, inboard, installing the fuel cells. The motor mounts coming out of

the firewall await an engine. There are a number of angle pieces sticking out, to which the nose attaches.

Aero-Tech in Santa-Fe Springs, California. The new tanks are lightweight and work well.

Installing the new fuel cells was not a simple matter. As Rich Palmer pointed out, the original rubber tanks were rigid while the new ones were soft and pliable, thus making the process of fitting the original tanks (in particular, the main front tanks) a complex task. They had to be hung and not simply stuffed by hand into the space provided.

The shape of the tanks is unusual, with all kinds of angles that had to fit exactly into the allotted space in the main spar. To make the job easier, foam was cut into strips and inserted into several of the tanks, giving them a new rigidity. However, in the tank that contained the fuel float, foam could not be used because it would inhibit the movement of the float. Foam is not dense and takes up less than one percent of fuel space. It is fuelproof, fireproof and even inhibits explosions in case of a heavy impact. But in this case it was used to give the fuel cell its shape.

Fuel cells were installed in the leading edge of the wing but they were not hooked up. As it is presently outfitted, the P–38 has a total fuel capacity of 300 gallons, giving it a flying time, at cruise, of about 2½ hours—about half the stock P–38's range. Drop tank pylons were rigged under each wing, but the tanks have not been fitted.

All the original aluminum fuel lines were badly corroded and had to be replaced. Once again the originals were used as templates for new aluminum lines. The fuel lines on the engines were replaced with new braided lines and up-to-date fittings and connectors were used throughout.

The firewall is mild steel forming a barrier between the engine compartment, and the soft aluminum structure of the rest of the plane. If there was a fire, this would help prevent it from causing structural damage. The area right behind the oil tank is removable. The oil tank and the firewall must be removed to adjust the control cables. The wing attachment knuckles are on the right side of the photograph. On the unit protruding above the firewall is a coolant line that goes back to the radiator between the skin of the aircraft and the landing gear compartment. Kevin Eldridge has installed some of the old lines here to see where everything goes so that copies can be made. Some of the Army-Navy (AN) fittings are visible on the firewall.

Rebuilt "yellow-tagged" fuel pumps replaced the originals, and a new aluminum fuel-selector switch was installed in the cockpit.

Finally, rebuilt carburetors were fitted to each Allison.

Fighter Rebuilders chose not to install a fire extinguisher system because the risk of fire is fairly remote, considering their track record. (The only major safety problem they have had so far has been a generator that exploded on their P–47, filling the cockpit with heavy smoke, smoke so thick that the pilot could not even read the instruments. In spite of the smoke, he was able to safely land the airplane after opening the canopy and lowering the gear.)

The starboard engine prior to being installed in the aircraft. The motor mount structure (a strong aluminum forging) is shown in the background. The right-hand side of the motor mount attaches to the outboard wing section, which hasn't been installed yet—that is why it is unsupported. John Kagihara is working on the nose, and you can see the freshly overhauled oil tank mounted on the firewall.

The starboard engine is installed and this picture gives a good idea of how the engine fits onto the engine mounts.

Part of the original fighter nose has been installed as a mock-up for the new one.

Also, the cockpit itself is substantially protected by a steel firewall between it and each engine compartment. (Rich Palmer pointed out that during World War II only bombers were outfitted with fire control systems.)

Landing gear overhaul

One of the first objectives of the disassembly process was to remove the landing gear. Once it was off, the major components were thoroughly cleaned by means of a glass bead blaster that removed all the rust. Then they were set aside in a corner of the shop for reinstallation at a later date.

All the components of the landing gear system were thoroughly checked out by Menasco Overhaul, rebuilt where necessary and then delivered back to Fighter Rebuilders. The gear was reinstalled while the airplane was still outside and then as the winter weather approached, it was pushed inside the shop (both wings off) for the completion of the rebuild.

While the plane was up on jacks in the shop the landing gear was put through a swing test to make

sure it was working properly. Clearance in the main gear well is minimal with only a quarter of an inch clearance between the wheel as it retracts and the inside of the landing-gear well. The tire frequently rubs and there were scuff marks inside the well and on the side of the airplane after one or two tests. The roof of the main gear well is dimpled for clearance so the tire can fully retract.

"This is a tricky area," said Rich Palmer. "For example on the Mustang, there are fuel lines in the wheelwells and you have got to make sure that every-

Next page
A close-up of the starboard series 111 motor. Its crankshaft rotates counterclockwise while port, series 113, crank rotates clockwise—a feature termed counterrotating. The counterrotating propellers cancel the torque reaction effect. This is early on during the restoration when the motor was hung. The engine exhaust system is partially installed, but the coolant lines, expansion tank, oil coolers and cowling formers are not installed. Pieces of the exhaust system rest on the floor below the engine, awaiting installation.

thing is where it should be because you don't want a tire rubbing against a fuel line when [the tire] is retracted. On the P–38 there are coolant lines and hydraulic lines up in there and that makes for a tight fit. We spent a great deal of time with shims to ensure that the main gear retracted exactly the way it was supposed to."

The gear doors also take a great deal of time to adjust properly due to their design. Again, in the words of Rich Palmer: "The doors are curved and all the hinges are different. The hinge just doesn't pivot in one direction. The hinge line actually moves at the same time that it pivots and so when the gear

doors open they actually move away from the airplane as they turn and then they suck into the airplane as they close. Getting everything to match up is important there.

"On the nose gear door on really early P–38s there was a similar arrangement, but then they went to a different system that allowed them room for guns and ammunition. They went to a system that had just one hydraulic actuator at the rear of the door and when they did that it became tricky because the door is so long and the fulcrum is so great that the front edge of the door would [stick] open slightly. Then they put a latch up there and if it

Joltin' Josie *halfway through restoration. The port engine has arrived from JRS Enterprises and awaits installation. Note the stainless steel shroud that is mounted above the oil tank. This shroud surrounds the exhaust pipes all the way back to the turbocharger, ducting cool air around the pipes to flush away the heat that would otherwise be trapped in the engine compartment. The* original nose has been temporarily fitted so that a new "photo nose" (without gun ports) can be built up by Mike McGuckian. The front windshield has been installed by John Kagihara and is covered by a protective plastic sheet. The pilot's seat is out of the airplane and is perched on the midsection of the port wing.

is not adjusted just right the door will creep open and so the potential is there for tweaking that door or bending its hinges."

Fighter Rebuilders spent a lot of time adjusting the fit of the landing gear and doors, but before the first flight they were operating perfectly.

Cockpit rebuild

John Kagihara and Rich Palmer both put a good many hours into the cockpit rebuild. The entire cockpit was gutted, checked for corrosion and then while it was totally empty the sheet metal was sanded, cleaned up and given a coat of Imron rust-inhibiting paint. The original multi-layered glass in the canopy had discolored and deteriorated with age and had to be discarded. New plexiglass was ordered for the windshield as well as for the windows. Kagihara spent countless hours on the canopy frames, cleaning them up, making new members where necessary, then fitting them together screw by screw.

The original engine control console was checked over and found to be in good shape as were the throttle control cables, so they did not have to be replaced. But many of the smaller vacuum and hydraulic lines were replaced as well as all the lines that route to the instrument panel.

Steve Hinton drew up a layout for a new instrument panel that gave him space to accommodate up-to-date navcom gear and a few other minor changes. Two separate navcom radios were installed as were a Loran system and transponder.

A new electric aileron adjustment control was installed in the center of the cockpit between the pilot's legs.

The pilot's seat was cleaned up and painted, then reinstalled, locating it slightly farther forward to allow more room for the passenger seat.

The Lockheed P–38 is probably the only fighter plane with car-style, roll-up windows. The window crank mechanism was checked and serviced and made operational.

Prior to the installation of the port engine on Joltin' Josie, *John Kagihara is shown installing some of the accessories that are easier to put in at this point, like the tach generator used to monitor engine rpm. The tachometer is actually a little generator bolted to the engine. The electrical current it generates goes to an instrument in the cockpit that is calibrated for the engine rpm.*

A view of the port engine, just prior to installation.

Getting the engine sling ready for hoisting. John Kagihara checks the motor mount. Rich Palmer is checking hardware just aft in the engine, making sure all the right nuts and bolts are ready.

Steve Hinton, driving the fork lift, gently eases the port engine into place. Kevin Eldridge is looking in at the aft part of the engine, checking alignment, while Rich Palmer is at the front, stabilizing the motor. JK is on the ladder on the other side. One of the motor mounts from the outboard side, that attaches to the wing, is swung down to accommodate the engine installation. With the inboard side of the engine situated and in place, the inboard motor mount is already swung back into position.

Lining up the port engine so that it can be bolted to the engine mounts. Left to right: Hinton, JK, Mike De Marino and Rich Palmer, who has thrust a bar into the front engine mount hole to help line up the heavy Allison.

The engine is being centered and aligned so the bolts will fall down into their various holes. DeMarino is on the outboard side of the engine, pushing. JK is standing above to drop the bolts home.

When they were finished with the cockpit, everything looked brand new; they had even made new knobs for the throttle controls. A new fuel selector control was fitted to the left of the seat, and the cockpit seemed roomy, with excellent visibility.

Rollout

Work on the rebuild went on steadily until the spring of 1988, when enough had been done inside and it was necessary to get the P–38 outside so that the wings could be installed and the airplane could be painted. A lot had already been accomplished: both Allisons had been installed, a lot of the electrical system had been fitted, the hydraulic system had been installed, much of the control system was in, the cockpit was halfway there and the canopy and cockpit glass were complete.

A fork lift was used to fit the wings back onto the fuselage: "Basically you just slide them into the airplane so that the big knuckles are engaged and once you get them lined up, you start shoving pins and

Hanging the port motor. The two front holes on the engine mount are slightly oversize, while the rear holes are just the right size for the bolt.

The port engine's bolts are installed and the fork-lift truck has pulled away. Bolts are being tightened down.

The top of the right-hand wing, showing the extensive sheet metal used to shield the exhaust system from engine heat.

bolts home, rocking it back and forth," said Rich Palmer.

"There are three different systems that enable the wing to be attached to the airplane. The big knuckles (bathtub fittings) for the spar are attached by two large pins. Eighteen smaller bolts attach the wing to the fuselage. Four bigger bolts attach the rear spar. The outboard engine mount fits onto the leading edge of the wing, plus all the fairings.

"It's not as simple as having part A and part B and just fitting them together," said Palmer. "There is lots of flex. You are jumping up and down on the wing and then there were guys on the wing tip pushing it one way and then another way. Finally, it all came together."

A lot of work was still ahead, however. The wings needed to be attached; the electrical system had to be completed; the propellers had to be attached and tested; the ailerons and flaps needed to be hooked up; the cockpit needed to be finished

An overhead view of the starboard turbocharger bay showing the exhaust pipe, heat shrouding and where the center section of the shiny, replacement sheet metal has been fitted to replace the corroded metal around the bay. You can also see a P–51 wing in the jig at the left. Alan Wojciak is talking with Mike McGuckian, and Browndog, the shop's mascot, can be seen at the far left of the picture, asleep in his chair.

The turbocharger units that came out of Stephen Grey's P-38—they are virtually destroyed. The one on the left has lost all the metal around the turbine wheel. On the right-hand unit, the exhaust portion is gone.

John Kagihara is installing some of the parts that surround the exhaust system. In the foreground are pieces of stainless steel that wrap around the turbocharger area.

The large orifice is where the exhaust from the Allison engine exits. On stock P–38s with operative turbocharged engines there was a butterfly valve inside the exhaust pipe that could be closed by the pilot and this would route exhaust through the turbos, spinning the turbine to produce extra boost. At low altitudes the butterfly valve would be in the open position because the extra boost was not needed but as soon as the butterfly closed, exhaust would be forced into the turbos and out through that ring beneath the fin. The ring and the flying saucer-like plate on top are known as the turbine bucket. On Joltin' Josie the turbo system was inoperative thus there was no butterfly valve in the exhaust pipe. Turbo systems can be a lot of trouble and Fighter Rebuilders decided that from the maintainence standpoint they were better off without it.

83

and the instruments needed to be tested with the engine running; the nose needed to be finished; and the airplane had to be weighed and its balance point located so that the appropriate amount of ballast could be added. The fuel systems and hydraulics, cooling and oil systems all had to be run for the first time. With all this yet to be done, the

pressure was on to complete the rebuild in time for its debut at the Oshkosh 1988 air show. First flight was still a month away.

Like a musician playing an instrument, Kevin Eldridge is shown in the course of his work, fabricating hydraulic tubing for the P–38's system. There must be close to a thousand feet of these lines in one airplane, and every piece had to be made by hand. Once a line was fitted to Josie, another was made to match it for the second P–38 rebuild under way at this writing. There are probably 500 separate lines in the Lightning.

Looking down on the exhaust system from the top of the boom. The projection at the top of the picture is where the turbo fits. The raised sections along the tube are the clamps where the individual sections are screwed together. The two scoops on the side had different purposes. One ducted warm air to the cockpit where the pilot could adjust the cockpit temperature by controls along the side of the windshield. The other scoop ducted air to a vent on top of the turbo to cool the turbine blades. Rich Palmer pointed out that early P–38s (up to the H model) used hot air from the right-hand engine to heat the cockpit and air from the left-hand engine to heat the nose. Later models used air from both engines for cockpit heat with electric heaters in the nose. However, on Joltin' Josie all these systems were removed during the rebuild and are no longer operative.

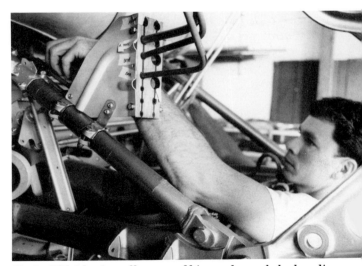

Kevin Eldridge installs some of his newly-made hydraulic lines. The lines go out to the engine area to run the landing gear on the port side of the aircraft. In the foreground are the lines coming into a wooden vise that he uses as a guide to hold all the lines together. Behind it are the bell cranks and the rods that control the mixture, throttle and propeller settings.

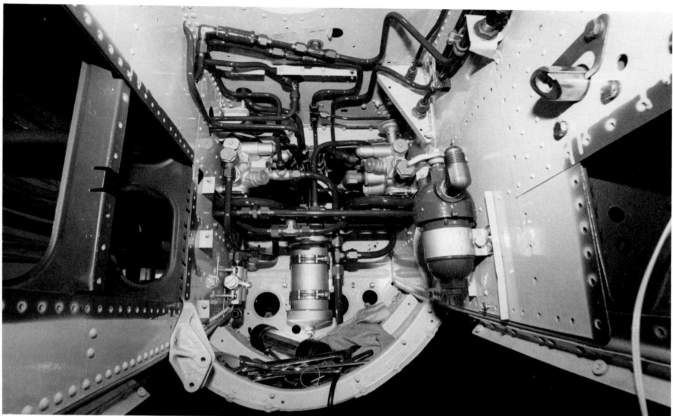

Looking aft inside the nose landing gear bay, the landing gear uplock pin can be seen on the upper right on the wall. This view shows well the number of hydraulic lines— many with several complex bends—that Kevin Eldridge fabricated. The valve on the right controls the raising and lowering of the landing gear and runs off a cable that goes to a control arm in the cockpit. Two similar valves (to the left and right of center) are flap-operating valves, again run by cables and connected to a control arm in the cockpit. The landing gear and flap controls are hydraulically assisted and could never be operated manually and therefore an accumulator from a P-51 (shown in the lower center of the photo) is fitted. Its purpose is to keep up a pressure of, say, 500 pounds per square inch in the hydraulic system, so that in an emergency there would be a certain amount of hydraulic pressure to aid in the operation of those controls. It would have been too expensive to rebuild the P-38 unit, therefore the P-51 unit was installed. The hydraulic filter for the system is also on the right.

Kevin Eldridge works on hydraulic line installation.

The gear was tested once again after the plane had been rolled out, and a whole afternoon was devoted to checking the retraction mechanism. The gear comes down rapidly and with considerable force. You want to be sure you are well clear of the wheel as it comes down and locks in place.

The rebuilt prop motors were installed as well as the brand-new hydraulic accumulator from a P–51 and an electric trim tab adjustment. As Steve Hinton pointed out, "This is the only P–38 with an electric trim tab adjustment."

Wing rebuild and installation

The wings of the P–38 had been removed many years before when the airplane was originally moved to Ontario, California. Even though they were refitted, they were never fully and completely reinstalled. They were on there "just for looks," remarked Rich Palmer.

The flap system, had been ailerons and wing tips were removed so that the inside of the wings could be carefully inspected and repaired where necessary. The leading edges of the wings had some hangar damage from people climbing on the wings or accidentally hitting them over the years and also needed repair.

After both wings had been cleaned and thoroughly checked, they were reassembled outside the

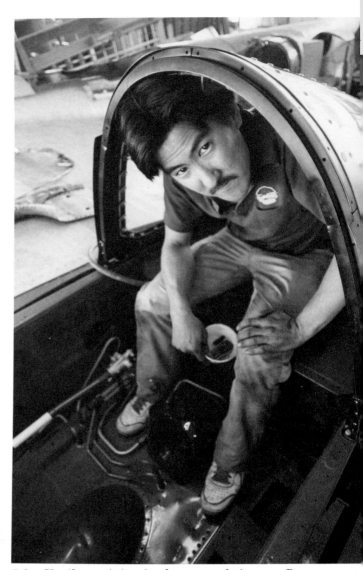

John Kagihara sitting in the rear cockpit area. Between JK's feet is the emergency hydraulic tank. When the rear seat was put in, a new one was made and installed in the nose. During World War II this area housed radio equipment; today, Josie can accommodate a passenger. And although you have a great view of the pilot's helmet, you can also see out the sides and forward through the side windows. It is a quiet ride compared to other warbirds, because the exhaust runs through all that ducting plus the gutted turbocharger housing. There is none of the coughing, sneezing and loud popping you hear from the Mustang's Merlin or a big radial engine. Everything is quiet and smooth. But a ride in the passenger seat is like bending over to tie your shoes: for however long the ride lasts, it is not comfortable. With just a small amount of turbulence, your head bounces off the canopy. (The seat is actually forward two inches or so, but still there is no headroom at all. The main wing strut goes through below the seat so the seat cannot be lowered further.)

Steve Hinton working at his bench in his usual mode of doing two things at once. The electric propeller controls, which bolt on to the front of the propeller and control the pitch of the blades, are on the bench in front of him. Note the LA Lakers hat; everyone at Fighter Rebuilders seems to be a Lakers fan.

Steve Hinton's "spaghetti"—part of the electrical wiring. Every piece of original wiring was taken out of the aircraft. The reason for this was that the aircraft had been used for training at a mechanical engineering school, so it was not known what had or had not been done to it. Its age alone, however, was reason enough to redo the wiring.

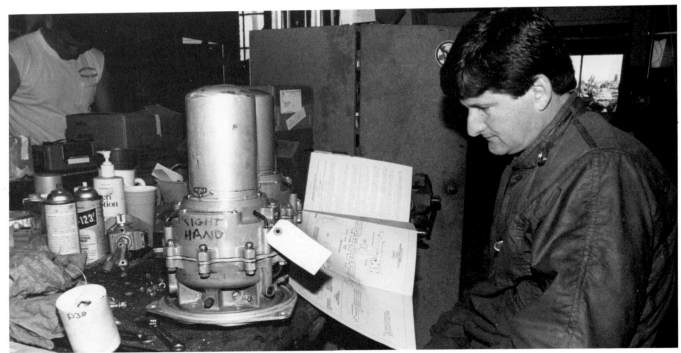

Steve Hinton consults the schematic of the starboard electric propeller control unit. Most warbirds had hydraulic propeller controllers, but the P–38s were electric.

Original factory erection and maintenance instructions manuals were used during the rebuild. Here, the dash four manual is open to a diagram of the cooling system for the port engine from the firewall forward. The picture shows only the contours of the cooling system, the two separate lines that come from the front of the cylinder head, and the header tank which serves as a reservoir and expansion tank. A dash one manual was for pilots, while dash two, three and four dealt with structure and maintenance of the airplane.

shop and preparations were made for reinstalling them onto the airplane. The elaborate flap mechanism then had to be adjusted. There are four flaps with eight adjustments for each flap! All the flap components had to be rebuilt and reinstalled in the outer wing panels before the wings could be attached to the airplane.

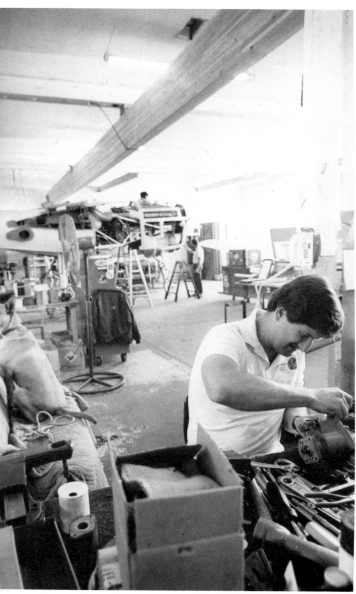

Fighter Rebuilders had to expand the shop in order to work on the P–38. The shop was of World War II vintage and was actually used as the Cal-Aero Flight Academy engine overhaul shop. Fighter Rebuilders reconfigured it into a hangar. They had to remove the building's 50 year old support posts to make room for the P–38 to fit in the shop. The large beam near the ceiling replaces the support posts by supporting the roof. Browndog watches.

Fighter Rebuilders had a stock of P–38 radiators, and prior to the rebuild they went through them and pulled out the best of them for Josie. They were checked for leaks and in this photo Rich Palmer is fitting sealing strips to a radiator that is just back from being cadmium plated. While at the cad-plating shop the original sealing strips were lost and new ones had to be fabricated. At the bottom left of the picture is an exploded view diagram from the maintenance manual.

The radiator area on the port boom. The system has been completely assembled and ready to be covered with ducts. The coolant lines have been installed and the hoses double-clamped for safety. The radiator is held in place by a steel band around its perimeter. The steel band is attached to the boom by the turnbarrels that are shown at the top and bottom of the radiator. The return line, below, combines with another in the main wheelwell. Also shown are the four control cables to the rudder and elevators, and a thinner cable for rudder trim. The inspection hole shown below the radiator is known at Fighter Rebuilders as the "Hell hole." The Fighter Rebuilders crew sometimes spends hours inside these claustrophobic spaces. The four lugs are for the Dzus fasteners that anchor the sheet metal shroud.

Previous page
This photo of the main-gear well shows the high quality of rebuild. The large, dark metal tube is a main coolant line from the radiators to the engine.

John Kagihara and Rich Palmer holding a new fuel cell made to order for the P-38. It is an inboard fuel cell and its capacity is 60 gallons (US). It will be stuffed into the cavity between the port engine and the cockpit nacelle. The outboard cell goes in next to it, and the two are interconnected. At the bottom of the cell you can see a sort of step or cutout to allow clearance for the engine controls from the cockpit.

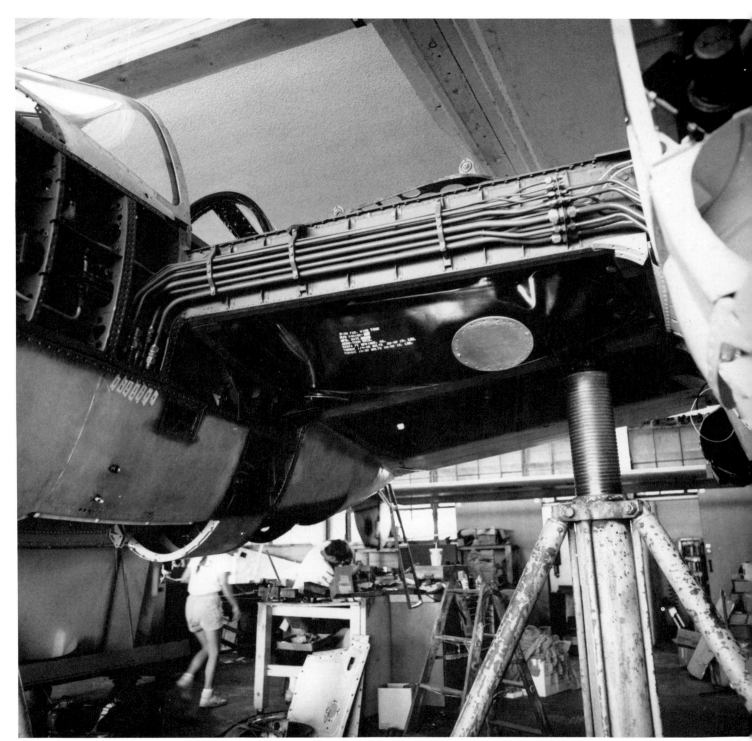

A view of the leading edge of the inboard wing. New hydraulic lines are all installed. The front fuel cell is shown installed and hanging in the bay. The original tanks were so thick and hard, they held their shape.

Because the new fuel cell is made of thinner material, it does not do so, and lugs had to be designed and made to hold the tank in place.

Steve Hinton installing the cover plates on the starboard reserve fuel cell. The cover plates are necessary to gain access to the interior of the tank to service or repair the points where the fuel lines attach to the tank. After the cover plates are on and all is tight and fully connected, the stress door is installed. The stress door is a structural part of the airplane that encloses the fuel cell. It is different from a simple access panel, which is not a structural part of the plane.

Alan Wojciak, a sheet metal expert at Fighter Rebuilders. Here he is working on a component for a P-51 Mustang, with the P-38 in the background. Fighter Rebuilders is usually rebuilding several warbirds at any one time.

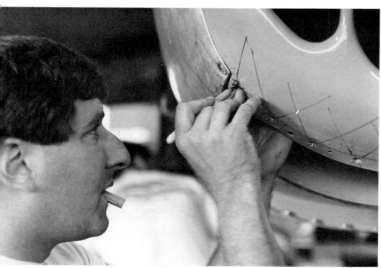

John Hinton getting ready to install the new sheet metal that was made to replace the steel on the bottom of the engine cowlings. He aligns the sheet metal with the nut plates, marking the exact places to drill holes in the sheet metal.

John Hinton working on the sheet metal stiffeners for the bottom engine cowlings on the Lightning. This photograph symbolizes the countless hours of careful handwork that went into the rebuild. Bob Pond suggested that overall cost of the rebuild went into the high six figures.

The starboard motor showing the cowling stiffeners installed. The spinner backing plate is on, and the electrical brush contacts for the propeller are in place around the propeller shaft.

Work in progress, with the original nose pieces in place so that templates can be made for fabricating a new nose.

A view of Fighter Rebuilders and Planes of Fame Museum from the air. Joltin' Josie *can be seen in the left center with her distinctive striped paint scheme. Fighter Rebuilders is directly off of the port wing, and directly opposite* Josie *is the Planes of Fame main hangar. Parked in front of the hangar is John Sandberg's Reno racer,* Tsunami, *flown by Steve Hinton. To the right of the B-25 in the lower corner of the photo is a dual-control P-51 Mustang that has just been rolled out of Fighter Rebuilders and awaits its first test flight. This picture was taken from Reeves Callaway's Gazelle helicopter.*

Right-hand engine is in, and the left-hand engine is ready for the fork lift to move it. The nose pieces are original but are being used only as templates so that a new "photo nose" can be fabricated for the airplane's restoration.

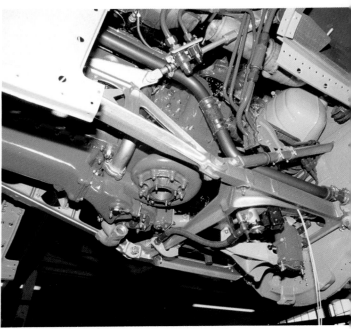

Looking up into the back of the starboard engine area. You can see the oil tank and the maze of brand-new coolant and hydraulic lines.

Landing gear retracted into the wheelwell illustrates what a tight fit it is when the tire and wheel are installed.

Prior to the wing attachment task, JK studies the main spar area, carefully planning how to attack the job. Note the flap control cables hanging down. In the background are two of the museum's aircraft, the T-6 and the Douglas Skyraider.

The nose gear on the P–38 includes a so-called shimmy damper which contains an air reservoir. The entire nose gear is under pressure when it retracts so that it retracts perfectly straight into the narrow nose gear well, where tolerances are tight.

Kevin Eldridge pours fresh oil into the starboard engine. Each tank holds 13 gallons.

The left-hand engine prior to the first taxi test. The nose is
still not complete.

Takeoff on Joltin' Josie's first test flight. The first flight
was in the early evening of July 22, 1988. Fighter
Rebuilders prefers to make most of their test flights in the
early evening, when there is less traffic and visibility is
good. Steve Hinton is accelerating down the runway and
will be airborne in a few more seconds.

The P–38 seen from underneath, as Steve Hinton overflies the photo plane, the museum's P–51. The thin, cloud-like strips are actually reflections from the P–51's canopy.

Steve Hinton flies the P-38 to Oshkosh, 1988. The picture was taken from the B-25 belonging to Bob Pond. Stan Stokes

A photo of Joltin' Josie *at the 1988 Oshkosh Air Show, its public debut.*

May 1989, Joltin' Josie *finally is ready for a paint job.*
Rich Palmer

With the museum's Me 109 in the background, Joltin' Josie *gets a proper full paint job in May of 1989, almost a year after the first flight. Color choice was silver, and rather than leave the airplane in a natural unfinished* state (as was the case in wartime) it was considered better to give it a good coat of protective paint against corrosion. Rich Palmer

The starboard engine is run up following repairs, May 1989.

May 1989, the P–38J gets a new paint job. Here is a close-up of the right-hand rudder.

Mike McGuckian making a new part for the nose. The original pieces of the nose were used to make a template; the template is then used to manufacture new pieces. The template or form block on the bottom is made of pressed wood cut to the shape of the piece to be made. The top of the template is plywood cut to the same shape. Metal is sandwiched between the wood pieces and hammered down around the lower form block. The part is then removed from the form block and is sent away to be heat-treated and hardened. Production line machines can stamp them out by the thousands, but for Fighter Rebuilders, these are individually crafted by hand. On the left is the machine gun mounting structure.

Work continues on the P–38's nose as Mike McGuckian considers his next move. Some of the new skin is in place on the bottom.

98

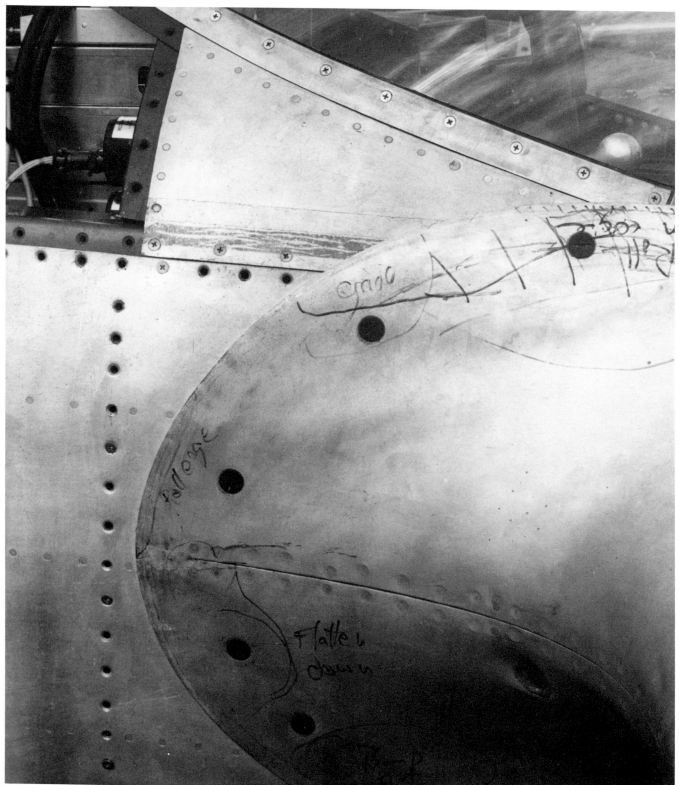

Rich Palmer has written notes to himself on the metal of the P–38's wing fairing to remind himself of things that need doing. On the prototype P–38 there was no fairing, but after extensive flight testing, Lockheed test pilots discovered that compressibility problems caused the nose to tuck under. This was almost completely eliminated by the careful fairing of the wing to the cockpit nacelle on production aircraft, as shown here.

A close-up of the left nacelle of the engine. The cowling has been fitted, and original pieces are installed. The original cowling was badly damaged—particularly the top pieces from being walked on over the years. The aluminum alloy used then was softer than today's, so the old panels rolled out easily, back to their original form, on an English wheelroller. Steve Hinton and Kevin Eldridge are working in the wheelwell.

This photo of the inside left landing gear well, looking aft, shows part of the complex landing gear door retract mechanism. The shuttle valve to the right of the pulleys opens and closes the gear doors. As the landing gear retracts, it pushes the valve, closing the doors and vice versa. The cables run forward, through a pulley on a track which is connected to arms that open and close the front portion of the landing gear doors. On the left is a 1¼ in. coolant line between the skin of the well and the exterior skin of the aircraft that carries coolant to a radiator. The hole for the 2½ in. coolant return line can be seen to the left of the carriage. The 4 x 6 in. access holes do not allow much room to work.

A Fighter Rebuilders employee studies the main gear doors. Making these doors close tightly and perfectly each time was a challenge due to the fact that the complex closing mechanism is difficult to adjust. You can see the many holes drilled in the interior panels for lightness.

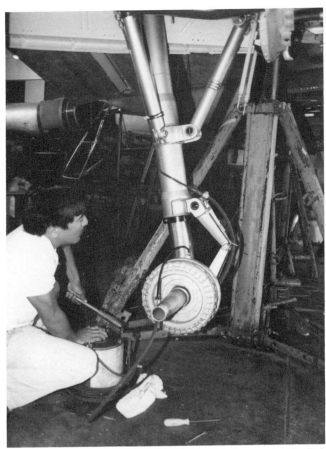

John Kagihara bleeding the brakes. This is a multiple disk brake unit mounted on the axle. It has several disks inside it; some rotate with the wheel and some are stationary. When the pilot presses the brake pedal, hydraulic pressure presses the disks together. The early P–38s had a shoe type brake, but it was not powerful enough for such a fast, heavy fighter.

Kevin Eldridge kneeling on the left and JK on the right, installing a wheel. The tire is an older type with a diamond tread on it. These were used for the first few flights, then were changed over to a newer style of tire. The control arms seen hanging down from the gear well close and open the landing gear doors.

A view of the port side main landing gear including tire and wheel, as JK works on the canopy in the background. The "scissors" is on the right. Crucial to the operation of the gear is a micro switch on the scissors which is connected to a mag-solenoid switch in the cockpit that functions as a safety switch to prevent the gear handle from being pulled while the plane is on the ground.

102

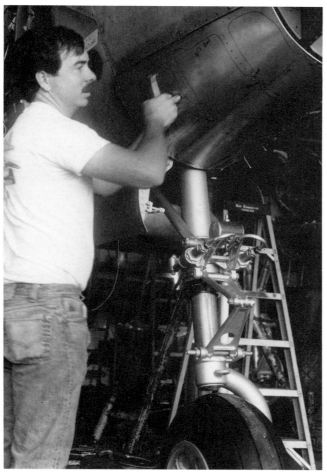

Mike McGuckian working on some of the new skins. This photo shows some of the interesting features of the nose landing gear. A brand-new tire is obvious, but to prevent oscillation at high speeds there is a shimmy dampener, right above the scissors. The dampener's reservoir is pressurized to 15 psi. This pressure causes a couple of small actuators to rub against bumpers that keep constant pressure on the sliding shaft of the landing gear. The pressurized hydraulic fluid dampens any oscillation in the wheel by keeping pressure equal on both sides of the shaft. The steerable front landing gear strut has another feature built into it: as the plane lifts off the ground, the strut centers itself. This is important, since the gear must not turn at all as it retracts into the wheelwell or it will not fit. At the bottom of the scissors is a tow bar attachment lug.

This close-up photo shows the reservoir for the shimmy dampener. The lines that connect the reservoir to the dampeners are not yet connected. Filling and pressurization instructions are on the reservoir. Due to the damage done in a towing accident, the nose landing gear had to be rebuilt. New gear arms were fabricated out of #4130 aircraft quality steel, but the original fittings were used.

John Kagihara working on the windshield, off the aircraft. All new plexiglass was made for the canopy. The metal strips that form the canopy were taken apart, overhauled, zinc chromated and then reassembled.

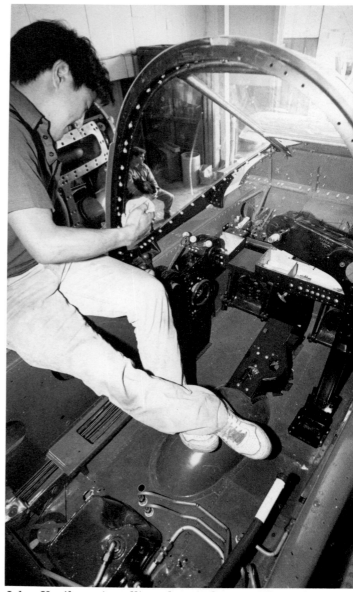

John Kagihara installing the windscreen. The rudder pedals at the front of the cockpit were taken apart and cleaned, greased and tested before reinstallation. The lever on the floor (painted red and white) operates the emergency hydraulic pump. The emergency hydraulic reservoir is on the lower left. To use this separate system the pilot presses the emergency hydraulic switch and pumps fluid manually to the hydraulic actuator, lowering the landing gear.

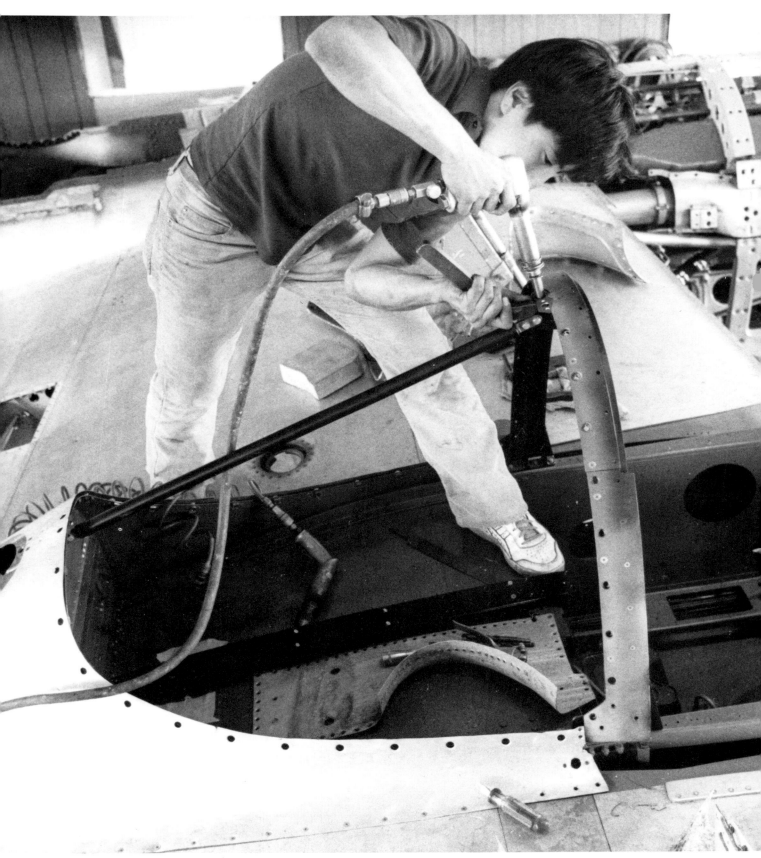

JK is riveting the aft canopy section.

JK is shown installing the rear canopy glass. Note the fuel filler hole in front of his knee.

Rick Palmer checks the fit of the side windows. These windows roll up and down as in a car. The original side windows were made of glass, but the new ones are plexi- *glass. They were not shaped to the exact angle the first time and didn't follow the tracks very well, so they were sent back to be reheated and reshaped.*

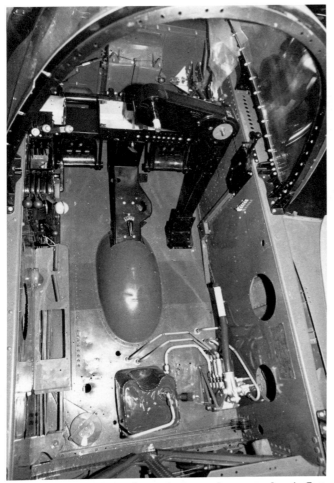

Looking toward the rear of the cockpit. On the upper portion of the picture you can see the rear top wing spar. Down on the left side of the floor is the emergency hydraulic system with Kevin Eldridge's handiwork visible. On the right-hand side is a large pulley that runs from the landing gear lever in the cockpit to the landing gear valve in the nose. The cables that go across the rear of the cockpit, in front of the spar on the right-hand side, are engine control cables that go from the throttle, mixture control and propeller control levers in the cockpit to the starboard and port engines. The thin cables in the center are trim control cables for the rudders and elevators. These cables were a nightmare for JK and Rich Palmer to install and adjust.

Looking down into the cockpit at the controls. A flap control handle is on the right cockpit wall, just forward of the windshield frame. Forward of the hump on the floor is the rudder trim. (The hump is for the nose wheel when it is retracted.) On the left-hand side of the floor are two handles. They are for fuel control, enabling the pilot to select which tank to use. Just above the forward fuel control is the landing gear handle. The white knob is actually two knobs and two levers that control the throttle for the two engines. The dark knobs next to the throttles are the propeller controls. Forward of these are two knobs with small lock buttons that control the mixture.

There is one lever inboard of the mixture controls that controlled an air filter. As cluttered as the landing gear wells were, there were large air filters installed in them for use in dusty conditions. The large holes on the walls are for the cranks for the roll-up windows.

JK holds up an instrument panel for a P–38. This is a stock panel and has all kinds of labels stenciled on it. This panel was not used in Josie; an entirely new one was fabricated to accommodate updated radio equipment, avionics and instruments. The updating was done in the interest of safety, efficiency and reliability.

A progress shot of the cockpit with space for the radios on the left. Some of the instruments are installed. The gauge that is lying on the floor is a hydraulic pressure gauge used for systems checks.

Just days before rollout, the pace quickened. Mike McGuckian is working on the nose. Kevin Eldridge and Rich Palmer are under the starboard engine working on hydraulics while Steve Hinton and an assistant are working steadily on the electrical system. No one was quite sure when the rollout would actually take place, but shortly after lunch on a Wednesday in mid-May 1988, Steve Hinton felt that everything was ready and the troops were called together to assist.

Joltin' Josie *is being pushed out by hand. Although it looks like it is being pushed back in, the crew is simply trying to take it down the ramp slowly. Steve Hinton is in the cockpit riding the brakes. The hydraulic systems have all been checked out except for the flaps. John Maloney and* John Hinton *push on the port side. The extra hands here are typical, as many "friends" of the museum drop in from time to time to lend their help or expertise. The propellers are not installed, and the leading edge of the inboard section has not been attached.*

Joltin' Josie's *starboard wing is shown during the cleaning process. Note the large amount of walnut shell dust. Less abrasive than sand or glass beads, ground-up walnut shells are used extensively in aircraft restoration for* cleaning sensitive areas. Later, during the first test flight, Steve Hinton had walnut shell dust flying everywhere as it worked its way out of the nooks and crannies of the P–38. Rich Palmer

The old and the new. An original portion of the flap area of the wing is shown next to a brand-new piece that is almost ready for installation. Note the large hole in the original component. Rich Palmer

A close-up of the same flap. It is so corroded that if you touch the area the metal simply flakes away, almost like a powder. This serious corrosion is from years of exposure to the elements. Rich Palmer

Prior to installation of the wings, JK in the yard at Fighter Rebuilders working on the left wing. The wing has been cleaned and stripped of all paint and corrosion. Note the slight droop on the trailing edge and the row of bathtub fittings—the knuckles for attachment to the main gear.

The port wing of the P-38 sits on stands in front of the Fighter Rebuilders shop during restoration. The wing is approximately halfway through the rebuild. Access panels to the inside of the wing have been removed so that all the interior areas can be cleaned and checked as carefully as possible. Often, a small dental mirror would be used to check obscure places. Note the unique bathtub fittings on the upper and lower edges. In the background is a Douglas Skyraider, minus its engine, awaiting rebuild.

113

The port wing is ready to be attached, and Jim Dale is working on the bathtub fittings prior to moving the wing into position. Note the drooping cables that will go into the wing once it is fitted into position. This photo emphasizes the massiveness of the Allison engine.

Installation of the port wing progresses. The fork lift has moved the wing closer and JK is on the stepladder, guiding it ever closer to the plane. The rest of the Fighter Rebuilders crew are busy with other tasks, but in a few minutes more muscle will be called in to persuade the stubborn wing to mate.

As Lefty and JK help guide the wing into place from the fork lift, a museum volunteer equipped with a crowbar and a can of WD-40 is on the top of the wing and is starting to jump up and down to persuade the bathtub fittings to come together as they are supposed to. This operation took the better part of an hour and in the end it was brute physical force that turned the tide.

Port wing installation almost over. The museum volunteer is using the crowbar at the end of the team effort to move the wing into place. The access panel on top of the wing is open so that flap control cables can be guided into place.

The port wing is finally in place and Steve Hinton tightens the screws on the aluminum fairing to make a snug aerodynamic fit to the wing against the port boom. Hinton is as much of a perfectionist as they come. He seemed to be as much in his element doing small detail work such as this or working on the electrical system, as he was flying the airplane.

The work continues after the wings are installed. Mike McDougall is working on the port boom by the radiator, laying out the invasion stripes. Bill Barclay is working on the port side by the turbo area, installing the bearings that go between the wing and the fuel cell. John Hinton is working on the starboard boom by the turbocharger. He is building the stainless-steel shrouds that surround it. Stainless steel is used here because it withstands heat better than aluminum. Lefty and Mark Foster are riveting the skin on the nose. Cowlings are off the engines, and a lot of nose panels are off for access. You can see the zinc chromate paint on the right wing where the leading edge was taken off. The wing tips are still on. In the background are the museum's various aircraft: the B–25 Betty Grable, an A–26 Invader, a Douglas Skyraider (that has since been restored), a T–6 and a P–40.

Steve Hinton in the cockpit after the attachment of the wings. He is moving the aileron to check that the control cables are correctly attached. The seat has not yet been installed. The shiny knobs are not stock, as the old aircraft had phenolic knobs on the throttles and new ones made of aluminum.

This photo shows JK installing some of the vacuum lines that go to the instruments. He is working through the access areas opened up around the windshield.

Kevin Eldridge fitting the radios and avionics. In his hand is a selector box for the radios. The top radio stacked on the wing is a Navcom, a navigational receiver that receives the VOR signals. The bottom radio is another VOR radio. This allows the pilot to tune one for the tower and one for air frequency. The second one down is a transponder which is required for flying IFR conditions. It lets the radar on the ground read the aircraft as a specific number rather than just a blip on the screen. The third radio down next to the bottom is a Loran unit. It uses signals from satellite and Loran radio stations to calculate for the pilot his position in latitude and longitude down to minutes and seconds.

Steve Hinton working in the cockpit, fitting the control wheel and hooking up the electric lines that come off of it.

Switches on the control wheel, originally used for guns, are now wired to run the radio and intercom.

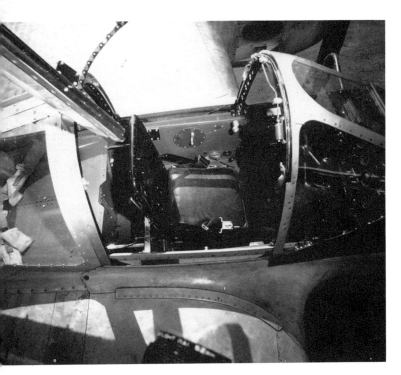

The nearly complete cockpit of the P–38, showing the cramped area behind the seat for a passenger. In production P–38s this area was used for radio gear.

This factory photograph of the cockpit of a Model P–38J clearly shows the gun sight at the top and the 20 mm cannon arming lever at the middle left. The gun sight is a heads-up display model, enabling the pilot to track his target while looking straight ahead through the wind- *shield. The two tubes at upper right are for cockpit air (primarily heat). Tony LeVier pointed out that the cockpit instrument layout changed a great deal from model to model. He was critical of the layout from the standpoint of cockpit ergonomics.* Lockheed

Rebuilding a warbird is all handwork—hours and hours of it. Here John Hinton takes a hammer to an obstinate piece of sheet metal near the end of the restoration.

A pilot's-eye view of the cockpit. The radio package is on the left side of the instrument panel. Just below the center of the control yoke are the magneto switches for the ignition system. Going across from left to right are the controls for the coolant doors, the battery switch actuator and lights and switches for the starter, including a wind-up and engage switch with boost pump for both engines. Behind the control yoke are switches for feathering the propellers. Controls also include a back-up system for adjusting propeller pitch. The large, round knob on the left-hand side of the console is the elevator trim, and to the left of it is the landing gear handle. One of the modifications on Joltin' Josie was an electric trim switch for the ailerons. Stock aircraft had cables running to the right and left ailerons to adjust trim. All that is gone on Josie. The electric trim control is the rocker switch right next to the rudder trim crank, on the floor between the pilot's legs.

Mark Foster (right) and Lefty (sitting in the nose) resume putting Josie's nose together. Kevin Eldridge on the ground, working on a hydraulic component. The wing fairing is removed in this photo.

JK is tapping out the nut plates and installing screws to attach the aluminum panels in front of the windshield.

Rich Palmer is on the ladder on the left-hand side of the photo, adjusting cables and the flap linkage inside the wing. Steve Hinton checks the progress.

Mike McDougall working on the port boom back by the radiators. He is using Bondo, filling in some of the minor holes and dents. Jim Dale is working on the exhaust shrouding around the port turbocharger. Right behind him is Bill Barclay, installing fairings, and Dennis Collins installing inspection panel covers.

121

At times the Fighter Rebuilders crew seemed like ants swarming all over Josie.

Two or three days prior to the first flight, the propellers were installed and the engines were test run. The gun doors are installed and a large part of the nose structure is built up and the skin is being put on. Much of the original nose's skin was steel. Over the years the steel had rusted around the gun ports, so aluminum pieces were made as replacements. The cone at the front of the nose was a steel piece as well. Steel was used because it was not a critical war material, easier to work with than aluminum, and it could withstand the heat of the guns. The cowling on the motors and the chin intake area where the intercooler and the oil cooler are located is one large unit constructed of steel. Many of the cowling formers were also made of steel. Steel skin was also used on the very bottom of the nacelles. It was badly rusted, so it was replaced with aluminum.

The original turbocharger intakes on the P–38 were rusted and badly damaged, so replicas were made from fiberglass. These are being fitted during the final days of the rebuild by two volunteers at Planes of Fame. Since the turbo-charger system on Joltin' Josie was removed, these dummy air intakes were fitted for cosmetic purposes only. Air for the engines now is ducted through scoops at the bottom of each Allison.

The empennage or rear section of the aircraft. The hold-down attachment to tie-down the empennage when the P–38 is on the jacks hangs down from the boom. The attachment points for the empennage to the boom are also visible here. It consists simply of a series of screws fastened all the way around the boom. Early-on in the production of P–38s, Lockheed engineers changed the angle of the horizontal stabilizer, resulting in the gap between boom and empennage. Over 10,000 P–38s were built, but the tooling was not altered, so the gap remained throughout the entire production run. At the upper left is the VOR antenna.

Inboard on the starboard lower vertical stabilizer is the designation and aircraft serial number. To the bottom section of the tail an easily replaced "bumper" section is attached. After a mission, with fuel and ammunition spent, the plane would be light in the nose and sometimes the tail would drag on landing; the bumper made it easy to repair any resulting damage. Josie's bumpers are fiberglass replicas of the original steel bumpers, which had rusted away. A shiny, new inspection panel stands out in contrast to the darker, pitted aluminum of the vertical stabilizer.

A close-up of the counterweight on the bottom of the elevator. The football-shaped section is lead, held on by a steel mount.

125

Chapter 5

First Flights

As the time for the first test flight drew near Steve Hinton remarked, "When it's all finished it will all have looked so simple."

But nothing was simple on this job. What would take fifteen minutes on a Mustang took two hours on the P–38, and pressure built to get the plane ready in time for its debut at the Experimental Aircraft Association (EAA) show at the 1988 Oshkosh airshow. *Josie* had already missed a date at a P–38 reunion in Texas in mid-May, but everyone knew that date was totally unrealistic.

Previous page
Mark Foster and Mike "Lefty" McGuckian continue working on the nose.

As Oshkosh grew closer, the pace quickened at Fighter Rebuilders. Hinton assigned more crew to the Lightning and for many evenings work continued on into the night.

Final assembly

Fabrication of the airplane's nose seemed to take the most production hours, and all those countless rivets were still being sent home only hours before the first flight. After what seemed like months of fabricating and assembling, it fit perfectly!

Another major task was adding ballast to compensate for the shift in center of gravity caused by omitting the heavy guns, ammunition and turbo chargers. *Josie* was carefully weighed to determine

Pushing the airplane is an all-hands effort. John Kagihara sits up on the wing. In the background is the Planes of Flame main hangar that houses the stars of its collection.

127

the exact center of gravity and then bricks of lead were added inside of the nose to move the center of gravity within design specifications. In the production P–38, Lockheed installed the battery in the port boom, while the starboard boom carried radio equipment. *Josie*'s radio equipment is now all in the cockpit and the battery was moved to inside the nose. These changes also helped compensate for the absence of the guns and ammunition.

Though eventually painted silver overall, *Josie* was left with a natural metal finish for the first flights. The yellow spinners and cowlings had been painted months before, but the crew worked frantically to apply the D-Day invasion stripes and national insignia before the first flight. At one point it seemed like each of the crew had a spray can in their hand. The nose art was not applied until just before Oshkosh.

Final adjustments were minimal because once the flap and aileron controls were set, they were set, and the aircraft needed to be tested in flight to see if they were set to their optimum position. As Rich Palmer said, "It's just a matter of letting Steve go fly it and see how it does."

Weight was added in the nose to balance the P–38, already having been weighed, to determine its empty weight and its proper center of gravity. From this, the amount of weight to be added to the nose is computed. A number of fighters like the Mustang had guns and armament carried right on the wings, at the center of gravity, but the P–38 is different with all the guns in the nose. Steve Hinton is melting lead into a bread pan and when the lead is solidified, it's popped out of the pan, holes are drilled in it and it's bolted into the nose of the plane for balance. On Josie *200 to 300 pounds were added.*

Lefty rivets the new aluminum nose.

Lefty seemed to spend all of his time building the nose of the P-38. On the day before first flight he is focusing intently on his handiwork—one of the thousands of rivets that he personally installed on Joltin' Josie.

Mark Foster files for a perfect fit the aluminum piece that surrounds the cannonport. The cannon actually slides back and forth on tracks inside the port to absorb the recoil when it is fired.

Painters lay out the stars and bars prior to painting.

Mike McDougall painting the invasion stripes on the booms of the P–38, just before the first flight.

The engines were run up to make sure there were no leaks and that everything was operating properly. Then Steve Hinton took it out for a taxi test with both engines running to get the feel of the controls with the P–38 in motion. It also gave him an opportunity to see if it tracked straight and to confirm that the shimmy dampener was functioning properly.

FAA inspection

Steve Hinton welcomed Jim Greene, the FAA inspector from Riverside, California, as a second set of eyes. "It never hurts to have someone else like Jim looking over our shoulder," said Hinton. "The FAA seems indifferent about warbirds. They have become more and more aware of them, and their broad rules allow them great latitude and discretion. In most cases they are very helpful because they realize that by and large these [restored] airplanes are really better than [the originals] were."

After checking *Josie* over thoroughly and watching as the Fighter Rebuilders' crew performed

Josie was given a quick paint job to enable Fighter Rebuilders to stay on schedule and fly the finished airplane to the 1988 Oshkosh Air Show. Here a museum volunteer is peeling mask off the painted white star. Later a full, first-class paint job was done.

another swing test of the landing gear, Greene licensed the P–38 in the special exhibition category. Essentially, he found nothing to complain about. Fighter Rebuilders' reputation is a good one and there were no surprises.

So with FAA approval, the serial number was painted on the Lightning's tail. A crowd of onlookers began to gather at Chino because the word was spreading that tonight was to be the big night for the Lightning's first flight.

The final hours

As work progressed, Hinton commented: "We normally try to schedule our first test flight at the end of the day because there is less traffic and the sun is low, giving us good visibility. It's an ideal time to take a ship up for the first time."

Finally, by 5:30 p.m. the nose had been completed, the radios and navigation equipment had been installed and the extra ballast to compensate for the missing guns and ammunition had been positioned in the nose. The landing gear had been cycled through numerous times during the afternoon while the Lightning was up on jack stands. The FAA inspector had departed, and the fuel truck was requested. Kevin Eldridge filled up the two oil tanks with fresh engine oil.

The fully restored port radiator area. The radiator doors are fully open to help cool the engines during the taxi-tests. The invasion stripes are painted and the stainless-steel shrouding around the turbocharger is finished (it is darker than the aluminum). Note the small slot along the leading edge of the radiator scoop as it joins the skin of the boom. This dumps the turbulence of the boundary layer air burbling along the skin of the aircraft straight through and out the rear, bypassing the radiator. This smoothes the flow of air through the radiator.

Rich Palmer refers to this as the adjustment phase. The plane is outside after rollout and some of the tools, including a curious looking vixen file for working on the complicated gear doors, are in the foreground. The plane is back up on jacks, even shortly before the first flight, as the pace picked up to get the plane ready for Oshkosh.

When the left wing flap is extended, as in this photo, it gives a good indication of how far aft and down the flap goes. This is the Fowler type of flap—an innovation of the day that increased wing area, lowering stall speed. The nonfunctional teardrop air intake is just there for appearance' sake. Also visible is the difference between the newly fabricated forward fairing piece and the original rear piece.

By 7 p.m. the tug with Browndog, Fighter Rebuilders' mascot, on board had towed the P–38 out onto the taxiway behind the museum. By this time the crowd had grown considerably. All the

Rich Palmer inspecting the flap system to make sure everything is operating properly. The system on the P–38 is different than those on most other planes of its day. It seems to have a million parts and it is a proverbial nightmare for mechanics to work on. On each flap there are eight cables to adjust and many other moving parts to maintain including a hydraulic motor with transmission and two jackscrews and various carriages and rods. Originally, an odd-size thread was used on the screw fitting on the end of the cable—approximately a 12/24 thread with a special 12/24 nut. These are not available anymore so these new fittings were specially made. According to Palmer, the whole system is terribly complex, and by WWII standards, many of these features were extremely advanced.

people who worked on the plane were there as well as a number of the financial backers. We were all full of anticipation and excitement as the big moment approached when *Josie* would be airborne again and the wheels would tuck up into the sleek fuselage.

More than 5,000 hours went into the rebuilding of *Joltin' Josie*. Many of these hours are volunteer hours; the shop crew is frequently joined by knowledgeable friends who are eager to help in the restoration. It's at the end of a rebuild, when the time for first flight comes, that a sense of extended family is felt strongly at Fighter Rebuilders.

First flight

The first flight was on the evening of July 22, 1988. Steve Hinton had his flight suit on, and a crew member had put his helmet on the wing for him as he began the pre-flight. His parachute also materialized—a disconcerting and sobering moment, for no one wanted to think that anything could or would go wrong.

Steve Hinton and Jim Greene, the FAA inspector, exchange comments just prior to first flight. Hinton welcomed his presence as a "second set of eyes." Greene found nothing to complain about and in fact complimented Fighter Rebuilders for the high degree of workmanship on the rebuild.

Jim Greene performing his visual inspection of the airplane. The paperwork is soon signed off and a set of operating limitations are drawn up. An "N" number is then assigned and the plane is legal to fly.

A final gear swing test being done in the yard at Fighter Rebuilders. The wheels go up and down with incredible force and you don't want to be in the way of one when they swing by. Rich Palmer noted that on the retract test you had to follow the book and be prepared to do lots of adjusting. The gear has to engage the up lock, then the sequence valve has to be adjusted along with every other component including the rods on the gear doors. Incidentally, hand pumping the landing gear down on the P–38 takes a lot of effort. Palmer said, "I think I'd rather bail out than have to pump that gear down by hand." The emergency hydraulic tank for the landing gear was moved to the front of the airplane when a back seat was installed.

The nose nearly completed. Workers and volunteers surround the airplane, readying it for the first flight.

Access to the P–38 cockpit is via a well-crafted chrome-plated folding ladder which when retracted, disappears into the rear underside of the cockpit pod. Hinton swung his foot into the bottom rung and lifted himself up onto the wing and from there took a few steps to the side of the cockpit, harnessed on his chute and eased himself in.

With Eldridge standing ready with a fire extinguisher, Hinton shouted out the inevitable "clear right!" and with a thumbs up from Eldridge, he pushed the starter button for the starboard engine. Slowly, the big blades began to turn. The Allison sputtered, whined and then burst into life, with a quick cough of white smoke as it moved into idle. With the starboard prop fanning the evening air, Hinton turned his attention to the port engine and in seconds it too came to life.

With both V–12 Allison engines going, the sound was like liquid thunder. The power seemed to be smooth and controlled. It was interesting to compare the sound of the P–38 to the P–51 Mustang. The P–51's Merlin engine has only very short, unmuffled exhaust stacks and sounds much more like a dragster, coughing and sputtering at idle. The long exhaust system on the Lightning tames the sound, giving it a more refined and stately note, not unlike the sound of a Rolls-Royce or Bentley motor car in a heightened state of tune.

Hinton cracked the throttles slightly and the air vibrated. You could feel the rumble in your gut. The drama on this balmy summer evening was accentuated by the crowd, many of whom by now had stuck fingers in their ears. Browndog backed away to the shelter of the tug as Hinton waved his arms to clear the taxiway. The wheel chocks were pulled as he gradually advanced the throttles until the airplane began to roll forward.

The P–38 was now rolling away from us at a good ten to fifteen miles per hour and we all made a mad dash for our cars as the Lightning turned the corner of the taxiway and disappeared from sight. We all rushed along behind in a ragtag collection of vehicles.

There must have been at least twenty automobiles and scooters lined up at the edge of the lighted runway. The rasping sound of a diesel-powered crash truck echoed off in the distance. Daylight was fading fast, and photography would be a challenge. At 7:35 p.m. the P–38 rolled into position to await takeoff clearance from the tower. As clearance came, the P–38's engines began to roar. Hinton released the brakes and twenty-nine Quebec began rolling. With both tachometers indicating 3000 rpm, the airplane shot down the runway and was airborne within ten seconds and into a gentle climb.

At 500 feet Hinton turned slowly to the east and came back around over the airport. The P–38 looked clean with no visible problems as he climbed higher. Over the San Bernardino Mountains a full

Kevin Eldridge does a last-minute polish. Note the highly polished area that is used as a mirror for the pilot to see if the landing gear is up or down.

An hour or so prior to the first flight, the fuel truck is summoned and the main tanks are filled. All of the final prep work has been completed. The nose is finally done. The invasion stripes have been painted on the aircraft and people finally have very little to do. Steve Hinton will be changing into his flight suit and the P–38 will be towed out to the ramp.

The tug pushes the P–38 out onto the ramp for an engine test prior to the first test flight.

Prior to the test flight, Rich Palmer checks the pressure on the P–38's shimmy dampener.

moon began to show and we could hear the Lightning off in the distance as Hinton gently sampled the plane's handling and surveyed the gauges on the instrument panel. He made a quick photo pass and then returned to the pattern. Daylight was almost gone and without a landing light it was imperative that he come in.

"Lockheed twenty-nine Quebec you are clear to land. Runway 21," came a voice in Hinton's headphones. The Lightning landed smoothly and effortlessly and taxied back to the air museum, followed once again by the convoy of automobiles now with their headlights on.

As the airplane rolled to a stop and the wheel chocks were put in place there were smiles on everyone's face. It was total darkness, and headlights and repeated strobe flashes were the sole illumination of the jubilant scene. Steve Hinton released the canopy latch and raised himself clear of the cockpit. With a broad smile, he jumped to the ground to do a brief postflight. There were handshakes and greetings from Rich Palmer and John Kagihara, the two mechanics who had put in the most time on the airplane. Then he was surrounded by well-wishers.

The postflight was short and the only squawks were minor: a pegged amp meter, a small oil leak and one generator was out. Considering the complexity of the restoration, it was a major accomplishment indeed.

The first engine run. Mark Foster is sitting on the wing of the starboard side of the cockpit watching for coolant or oil leaks. There is a transponder antenna on the nose just ahead of the nose gear. The wheels are chocked to prevent the aircraft from rolling when power is applied to the engine.

Both engines are running, and the generator is being adjusted. There is an electrical control to adjust the amount of voltage the generator puts out. The control was installed in the nose fuselage section, with access through the small door just above the nose gear door. Power needs to be run up enough to bring the generator on line before the voltage can be adjusted.

Checking systems after the engines are stopped. Dennis Collins is on the wing on the left-hand side. Hinton is on the right.

It's as if Hinton is saying "Have P–38 Will Travel." There is a story that the earlier P–38s, instead of having a ladder that swings down, used a stirrup. With the weight of the parachute, pilots typically would end up on the

ground, flat on their backs, so the early World War II pilots would hop up on the horizontal and walk up the boom to enter the aircraft.

As the celebrating started, plans were being made to go up again the following morning, for Hinton said it was necessary to calibrate the air speed indicator with another airplane. Joe Haley volunteered to take up the museum's P–51, and I volunteered to ride in the back seat of the Mustang to photograph.

Second flight

It was Saturday, July 23, 1988, another typical southern California day, smoggy but clear with minimal wind. Overhead, jets from the nearby Ontario airport could be heard as they departed the pattern. Celebrations among the P–38 team the night before had interfered with the crew's ability to get an early start for the speed calibration test, but by 8:00 a.m. the gate to the shop area had been unlocked and people were pre-flighting the Lightning and two other planes that belonged to the museum—the P–40 and the SNJ—which would also join us in the air.

The P–51 was rolled out of the main hangar and I followed Joe Haley to the airplane, camera-bedecked and excited at being able to have a go at my first air-to-air photography session. Around my neck hung the Canon T90 fitted with its 35–105 zoom. A second Canon A1 body with a 28 mm wide

Steve Hinton climbs into the aircraft for the first flight.

Hinton, with his "Let's get the hell out of here—do it!" type look.

139

angle fitted hung from my shoulder. My pockets were packed with extra film, both color and black and white.

I was apprehensive about my chances of successfully carrying off this exercise because the P–51 Mustang is not an ideal plane from which to photograph. From the back seat you sit low, with visibility restricted because the window ledge is practically at eye level. Thus my ability to shoot down and backwards was nonexistent. My quarry, the P–38, would have to be higher and slightly ahead for the best angle. Also, vision directly forward is limited, due to the pilot's helmeted head and once installed, I found myself looking directly at the back of Haley's helmet.

Haley helped me with my shoulder harness, and as he climbed in and settled in the driver's seat the sun began to bear down on both our heads. Something was wrong with the intercom switch and I was not able to talk with him, but we communicated successfully via hand signals. He left the canopy open until just before takeoff to permit ventila-

tion. The P–51 burbled and coughed like the proverbial dragster waiting to be unleashed at the green light as we taxied to the end of the runway.

Once again the Lockheed Lightning positioned itself at the beginning of Runway 21 and waited for clearance. The sun was high and the aluminum gleamed, the black and white invasion stripes giving the airplane a distinctive look. Then Hinton began rolling and was quickly out of sight, climbing up into the smoggy air. Haley advanced the P–51's throttles and we moved to run-up position.

Haley then pulled the canopy shut and announced over the radio that he was ready. Clearance came promptly and then it was our turn. Acceleration in the P–51 Mustang is impressive. Zero to 60 mph must be in the neighborhood of five seconds. The airplane is quick off the mark, quicker than the Lightning, and the kick in the stomach is noteworthy. I was glad I was strapped in snugly and part of the airplane.

The sensation is exactly like being in a super-fast sports car. Mix with that the third dimension of

The pre-flight check; everybody is looking at something. Steve Hinton is in the cockpit, preparing to start the engines.

140

flight plus the incredible maneuverability of the airplane and it is nothing short of impressive. We were airborne in seconds with the Chino airport buildings and runways passing beneath us on the right side. I strained at the shoulder harness and managed to get a few more inches of height as we climbed steadily toward our rendezvous with the P–38. That is the other thing about the P–51, its

Taxiing out for the first flight. Evening time, and Brown-dog is in his normal pose on the tug in the background.

smoothness. Only when it is taxiing does it seem rough and lumpy. In its element it becomes a totally different beast, exuding stark beauty and lithe aggression.

The passenger seat in the museum's Mustang is right over the radiator so that on wind-up for takeoff the cockpit gets warm. But there is too much to take in to worry about the slight discomfort of dripping perspiration.

Haley and Hinton were now talking on the radio as they moved to rendezvous at 5,000 feet. Meanwhile, I sat in the back seat of the Mustang in a state of euphoric shock, my fate in Joe Haley's hands. Below me the peaks of the San Bernardino Mountains north of Claremont and Ontario were clearly visible, barely pushing their way out of the yellow-brown haze of smog covering the southern California landscape.

As they talked to each other on the VHF radio I suddenly became aware of this "other world," the world of the aviator. I had flown many times before but never in a warbird. I was suddenly aware of why they do it. Listening to the chatter on the radio and then watching the two other planes form up on our starboard side was thrilling. I was a guest at a party celebrating the recommissioning of an airplane, and the celebrants were doing what they love— flying warbirds. I was aware of the challenge and the freedom of the skies.

Out of nowhere the Lightning suddenly emerged with the P-40 and the SNJ. The P-38 looked magnificent as the sun reflected off its pol-

Parading out for takeoff. Wherever the plane goes, everybody else wants to go. It is a typical first flight: anticipation builds, and everybody hears about it and wants to be there. The tower gets upset, but they've learned to take it as a matter of course at Chino.

142

ished wings and distinctive twin-boomed fuselage, both decked out with the stark black and white invasion stripes, first used for identification purposes in the D-Day invasion of June 6, 1944.

In the cockpit, Hinton appeared to be completely at home, the two mighty Allisons purring steadily on either side of him. Awaking to the reason why I was up there in the first place, I began to take pictures. As I clicked away with my two Canons, Hinton climbed slightly and we formed up on Kevin Eldridge's SNJ as he became flight leader.

Hinton and Haley compared air speeds as we cruised along at a steady 300 mph. Then Hinton gained altitude and passed directly over us. I fired away with the T90, knowing full well that if I came back with *one* special shot I would be pleased. (Later, as I looked over the proof sheets, I noted that my use of an excessively fast shutter speed resulted in a slight freezing of the props, giving an image that reminded me of the toy airplanes that I had played with long ago.)

It was Saturday morning in Indian Country, as one of my aviator friends refers to airspace up to 18,000 feet. There was lots of traffic and both pilots were advising each other of the numerous aircraft passing all around us. "Okay, Joe, I'm going up to 7,000 to play around a bit," and with that Hinton put the P–38 into a steep bank and climbed away from us toward the sun, its distinctive silhouette indelibly stamped in my mind's eye.

An action shot at the end of the first test flight as Steve Hinton makes a photo pass. The plane is about 70 feet above the runway.

With Fowler flaps extended, Josie *touches down for the first landing in well over 25 years. Landing lights are a blur.*

144

Celebration time right after the first flight; Steve Hinton is shaking John Kagihara's hand. A job well done by everybody. In the background are the "Looky-loos," the name the shop crew call the onlookers who come out to watch this part of warbird rebuilding. Matt Nightingale is to the left of JK.

Steve Hinton and Kevin Eldridge congratulating each other. Having just gotten out of the aircraft, Hinton still has on his Nomex flight suit and gloves.

Previous page
A view of Josie *from below and behind on the second flight. The photo was taken from the back seat of the museum's P-51 Mustang.*

Steve Hinton and the P-38 fly formation with Alan Wojciak and the P-40.

Joltin' Josie *was painted with black and white invasion stripes on the wings and booms. These stripes were used on* all Allied aircraft in the European theater on D-Day in June of 1944.

147

Joltin' Josie *in company with a T–28 over Chino, California. Note the smoggy southern California sky.*

Another view of Josie *in formation with the museum's P-40.*

The photo plane pulls in close to the P-38 during its second test flight. I am shooting from the back seat of the museum's P-51. The back seat is hot and I am using too *fast a shutter speed (note how the propellers are stopped) but am excited to be up in the Mustang and riding alongside* Joltin' Josie.

Chapter 6

On to Oshkosh

Departure for Oshkosh, Wisconsin, was scheduled for Wednesday, July 27, just five days after the first flight, and everybody turned their attention to prepping the Lightning for its first cross-country since it left the Air Force in 1946. Engine idle was adjusted, carburetors fiddled with, some engine bits moved to make the exhaust clean and on the night before its scheduled departure, *Joltin' Josie* was fueled and prepared for a pre-dawn takeoff the next morning.

Steve Hinton was up by 4 a.m. to rendezvous with the two other warbird pilots who would accompany him: Elmer Ward in a P–51 Mustang, and Dennis Sanders in the big Merlin-powered Fiat G59.

After a quick breakfast, Hinton climbed into the P–38's cockpit, adjusted the pedals and began the cockpit check. "With the airplane full of fuel, the reserve tanks are selected, the canopy is closed, battery switched to on, boost pump to on, fuel pressure is checked, and you make sure the landing gear handle is down," said Hinton. "You give the engine a couple of seconds, prior to starting wind-up, then wind up and engage the starter. The blades begin to turn and then the magnetos are switched on. You are using primer intermittently, until the engine is running and the mixture can be advanced. Looking over the gauges, I check to confirm that oil pressure is normal, and then the boost pump is turned off and I switch to mechanical. As the engine catches its breath, burbling and stumbling, like it always does, I make sure that the engine boost pump is working and then the same sequence is started on the other side.

"As the engines are warmed, I hold them to a thousand rpm until the coolant and oil temperature are both up (90–100 degrees and 75–80 degrees centigrade). Taxiing is no problem with the P–38 at a thousand rpm, but the brakes require very heavy pedal pressures which is typical P–38. I've flown two others and they were just the same."

The P–38 is an impressive beast with both engines turning, even at idle, and the sound is great. From the cockpit, Hinton remarked about the sound, a sort of undulating, repetitive "vrooming" that is music to warbird lovers' ears. Accompanied by the Fiat and the Mustang, Hinton taxied to Chino's Runway 21 and prepared for takeoff. When both engines were warmed up sufficiently and every-

thing was ready, he advanced the throttles to 3000 rpm, released the brakes, rolled down Runway 21 and climbed to altitude where his two companions joined up. The three warbirds were on their way.

As Hinton tells it: "We departed Chino, made a left turn and climbed to 11,500 feet, with our first stop to be Gallup, New Mexico. I've flown that route at least twenty times, going back to Minneapolis. I could probably do it without a map. The most difficult part is between the Colorado River and Flagstaff because of the terrain. Difficult in the sense that if you have a problem it's not always easy to find a place to land. It's not so much a problem with a twin but with a single-engined plane it could be tricky so we try to detour a little bit to make sure we have someplace to set down if we have a problem. Also, the higher you go the better your navigation aids work with their better range. And the higher you go the less traffic there is. You're out of the way of the Cessnas and things. Elmer and Dennis stayed close to me, 100 feet off my wing, and we would talk back and forth on our discrete frequency. Out of Chino, I looked over at Dennis and saw that a battery compartment door had blown off. So I said to him, 'Hey, Dennis, how come you're missing a big panel on the side of your airplane?' It had to be mailed to him at Oshkosh."

First stop was Gallup and the three warbirds refueled, checked their oil and were off again. But just after leaving Gallup, Elmer Ward's oil temperature began to rise and then his oil pressure began to sink. Hinton and Dennis Collins escorted the P–51 back to Gallup, and while the Mustang landed, they orbited the field for a few minutes until they realized that the problem would not be a quick fix and then continued on their next leg to Goodland, Kansas.

Hinton continued: "A cross-country is an excellent way to get a handle on fuel consumption. With the short hops that we do around Chino, it's virtually impossible to get a decent reading and that's another reason for going up to 11,500 for our cruising altitude. At 11,500 feet we were turning 2000 rpm at twenty-eight inches of manifold pressure and indicating 245–250 mph cruise. The Fiat had big drop tanks on it so we set our cruise to accommodate him. He cruised at thirty-seven inches at 3300 rpm. The fuel burn on the P–38 was exactly 100 gallons per hour. Two hours later we were at Goodland having a hamburger while the locals oohed and aahed and watched the warbirds tank up."

From then on it was a straight shot to Minneapolis and to Flying Cloud Airport where Bob Pond's collection is based. "The section lines run north-south and if you're thirty degrees to the section lines you know you are right on the money," Hinton said. He had phoned ahead and several hundred people were on hand as the P–38 and the Fiat rolled to a stop 6½ hours after leaving Chino.

By the way, do you have any idea what it costs to operate a P–38? When you figure in the insurance, fuel and oil, a figure of close to $1,000 per hour is not far off. Fuel is consumed at the rate of 100 gallons per hour, and at $2 or more per gallon this soon adds up. The oil is changed every twenty-five hours, and the two tanks hold thirteen gallons each. Insurance for the aircraft is approximately $8,000 per year. Routine maintenance calls for the cowlings to come off the engines every ten hours to check for leaks and so on.

Stan Stokes, aviation artist and friend of Bob and Jo Pond, continued with the story: "We spent the Thursday before Oshkosh painting the nose art

Joltin' Josie *with Steve Hinton at the controls on his way to the Oshkosh 1988 Air Show.* Stan Stokes

on and then repainting the nose, removing the blue paint and a few details like that. Then on Friday for the flight to Oshkosh we all got into Bob Pond's B–25, accompanied by his Yak. Steve Hinton brought the P–38 up close, and did some rolls around us, staying with us all the way to Oshkosh, about an hour's flight. It was a smooth flight, good weather and the P–38 looked great."

As the flight of warbirds from Minneapolis approached Oshkosh, Hinton mentally cinched his seatbelt tighter and focused all of his attention on the heavy airplane traffic around him. He had been to the Oshkosh fly-in before, and was prepared for the incredible amount of traffic generated in the skies for the event. Airplanes of all types and configurations come from around the world. It is like a huge international county fair. Instead of getting rides in a barnstorming biplane, though, you can purchase tickets for a short trip on the Concorde (which was parked next to the B–1 bomber). It is truly an aeronautical extravaganza and lasts for a whole week.

One of the highlights of the display at Oshkosh is the warbird section, and the star of the show was the Planes of Fame P–38 as it made its descent into the crowded airspace. With only two or three Lightnings flying in the world today, aviation buffs and particularly warbird fans light up with enthusiasm at its sight. The B–25, the Yak and the Lightning made a flyby before being cleared to land on the main runway.

"Everybody does an absolutely great job, the ground crew, the tower, you can't fault anything they do there, but for the pilots it's an event that requires total attention. The reason we went to Oshkosh was to have a reason to get the P–38 done, a goal, and we did it," said Hinton, after he had climbed out of the cockpit and shed his flight suit. He was obviously enjoying himself as he wiped down the airplane.

On the way to Oshkosh. Note that the nose gear door is not closed all the way. The new hydraulic actuator to close the nose door did not always work the way it should. Stan Stokes

Steve Hinton on final approach at Oshkosh.

It looks like a dead stick landing—falling out of the sky, with engines out. Actually, Steve Hinton is on final approach for his Oshkosh arrival and the camera shutter speed "stopped" the propeller's motion.

The P-38 with Steve Hinton in the cockpit taxis toward the warbird area at the 1988 Oshkosh Air Show. *Joltin' Josie* was the only P-38 in evidence at the fly-in, and excited warbird enthusiasts surrounded the airplane the entire time it was on display. Note the crowded conditions adjacent to the taxiway.

Steve Hinton emerging from the cockpit upon arrival at Oshkosh 1988. The stars and bars and the invasion stripes on the wing and the boom show nicely here. The fiberglass mock air intake is also evident. This angle gives a good view of the gear doors. The oil cooler outlet, through which the oil cooler air exits, is visible just aft of the propeller area.

154

Just after Hinton's arrival at Oshkosh. The plane is being pushed into position in the warbird display area. Hinton is in the flight suit. Owner Bob Pond is on the right.

Former P–38 pilots came out of the woodwork at the air show. I spoke with one gentleman who had actually owned a Lightning. There was another fellow who said: "You know, it was just after the war in

Volunteers help push the Planes of Fame P–38 into position at the annual 1988 Oshkosh fly-in.

A volunteer helps chock the airplane after its arrival at Oshkosh.

Steve Hinton wipes down some of the oil and grime accumulated from the flight, making the aircraft presentable.

At Oshkosh, the P–38 was one of the most popular attractions in the warbird area.

Kansas City. I was still in high school and there were two brand-new P–38s out at the airport. They were brand new; there wasn't a number on them and we could have had those for *$350 apiece*. I got seven of

my buddies together and we went out to the field in my old Terraplane and we ran in and there was only one P–38 still sitting there. I said, 'We want that one that's left,' and the guy said, 'Sorry, I sold them both and they're going to South America.'"

Bob and Josie Pond, who financed a good portion of the restoration. The tail of the Ponds' Yak, No. 27, is visible in the background—another warbird restored by Fighter Rebuilders of Chino.

Joltin' Josie participated in the warbird flyby, delighting the spectators with some aileron rolls. At the end of the weekend, Steve Hinton flew it back to Minneapolis. Two regional air shows were graced with the Lightning's presence before he headed home by way of Denver. On the way, he landed at McCook, Kansas, for fuel and then headed west. The P–38 was running perfectly when the port engine suddenly began to smoke, pop and bang, and pump oil out the engine breather. "I throttled it way back, but didn't shut it off. I would have if I had needed to but it quit smoking and throwing oil, so I left it in a simulated feather and landed at Centennial Field in Denver," said Hinton.

Repairs were made in Denver, and the Planes of Fame P–38 came home shortly afterward. Co-owner Bob Pond is building up hours in the airplane, and flew *Josie* to Burbank on the fiftieth anniversary of the first P–38 flight in January of 1989. Their plan is to use *Joltin' Josie* as a crowd-pleaser at air shows around the country, with Steve Hinton at the controls. Home base will be the Planes of Fame Museum at Chino, California, but *Josie* will spend

Steve Hinton talking to a friend at Oshkosh.

part of the year at Planes of Fame East, at Flying Cloud Airport, just south of Minneapolis, Minnesota.

Joltin' Josie *at Oshkosh.*

Joltin' Josie *at Oshkosh. Hinton is about to fire up the engines for a demonstration run.*

Bob Pond at the helm of Joltin' Josie, *named for his wife Josephine.*

*The P–38 with Bob Pond at the wheel taxies away from the
Planes of Fame Museum at Chino, California, on a flight
to Palm Springs.*

Joltin' Josie *just before acquiring a new paint job at
Planes of Fame. This picture was taken six months after
Josie's debut at Oshkosh.*